D1453961

Grudem Against Grace

*In Defense of
Free Grace Theology*

Grudem Against Grace

In Defense of Free Grace Theology

Robert N. Wilkin

Grace Evangelical Society
Denton, Texas 76202

To my good friends and co-workers:
Shawn Lazar, Bethany Taylor, Mark Gray,
Ken Yates, and Pam Esteven.

Contents

Introduction

Dr. Wayne Grudem is professor of theology and Biblical studies at Phoenix Seminary. He is the author of an influential and best-selling book on systematic theology.[1] He has written over twenty books, including books on a Biblical view of politics and Biblical manhood and womanhood.[2]

In this latest book, Grudem has decided to discuss the question of Free Grace Theology (hereafter, FGT).

I am delighted that he has done so.

In *"Free Grace" Theology: 5 Ways It Diminishes the Gospel* (hereafter, *5 Ways*),[3] Grudem calls attention to our views and to our writings. Thanks to Grudem, many more people have been exposed to the term *Free Grace*, and to some of our views.

However, this is not one of Grudem's best books. He has done a poor job of presenting and refuting FGT.

---

[1] Wayne Grudem, *Systematic Theology: An Introduction to Biblical Doctrine* (Grand Rapids, MI: Zondervan, 1994).
[2] He is the cofounder and past president of the Council on Biblical Manhood and Womanhood.
[3] Wayne Grudem, *"Free Grace" Theology: 5 Ways It Diminishes the Gospel* (Wheaton, IL: Crossway, 2016).

Grudem Claims He Does Not Believe in Lordship Salvation

Early in the Introduction, Grudem takes pains to say that he does not like the label *Lordship Salvation*. In fact, he hopes that, "no reviewer of this book will refer to my position as the 'Lordship Salvation' position, for I explicitly disavow that label as misleading and confusing" (p. 25). Instead, he prefers to call his position "the 'historic Protestant' position" or "the 'non-Free Grace' position" (p. 25).

The reason why he doesn't like the label of Lordship Salvation seems to be two-fold.

First, both sides agree that Jesus is Lord over all of our lives and the Lordship Salvation side admits that "our submission to Christ's lordship is imperfect in this life" (p. 23).

Second, he thinks that the Lordship Salvation label implies "that it is an unusual or minority view that seeks to add the idea of lordship to the ordinary idea of salvation" (p. 23).

Grudem may not like the Lordship Salvation label, but does it accurately reflect his theology? The fact that this book was endorsed by several of the biggest advocates of Lordship Salvation—including Drs. John MacArthur and J. I. Packer—suggests it does.

Moreover, as you read what Grudem says about the nature of faith, the condition of salvation, and the basis of assurance, you'll see there is no doubt that he is an advocate of Lordship Salvation.

Thus, rather than referring to his view as *the historic Protestant position* or as *the non-Free Grace position*,

I will stick with a title that is well-known and well-understood today—Grudem teaches Lordship Salvation.

Summary of Grudem's Arguments

Grudem believes that FGT diminishes the gospel. He does not claim we deny the gospel, only that we get some important things wrong. He makes his argument in five chapters.

In the first chapter, Grudem faults FGT for not adhering to what he calls *historic Protestantism*. He argues there was a consensus among the Reformers and others that while we are justified on the basis of faith apart from works, genuine faith must be accompanied by good works and a changed life.

In the second chapter, Grudem criticizes FGT for not making repentance a condition of salvation. He says that faith and repentance are two parts of one overall action (p. 45), therefore repentance is necessary to be saved. If you do not preach and require repentance, you are not preaching the gospel.

In the third chapter, Grudem addresses the question of assurance. Since genuine faith always results in good works and a changed life, Grudem thinks you can be somewhat confident of your salvation by looking to your good works. But without a pattern of good works in your life, you should not have assurance.

In the fourth chapter, Grudem claims that FGT underemphasizes trust in the person of Christ by teaching that faith is propositional. Instead, Grudem explains that saving faith means coming into Christ's presence, among other things.

In the fifth chapter, Grudem criticizes Zane Hodges for several key New Testament interpretations that Grudem claims are unlikely.

At least three other books have been published from a Free Grace perspective, answering Grudem's claims.[4] However, as Grudem recognizes, there is some diversity in FGT. In fact, there are some very important disagreements. We don't all have the same answers to the same questions. Hence, I think another book-length answer to Grudem is necessary.

Grudem's book is short. So is this one.

Moreover, I have answered Grudem's book chapter by chapter, and often heading by heading, so it is easy for the reader to follow along and compare arguments.

Grudem is happy to align himself with Protestant tradition. By contrast, I have often called myself a Biblicist. That means my highest authority is not tradition or confessions, but the Bible. I hope that comes across in this text.

Grudem is very concerned that we have not followed the Protestant confessions. In fact, FGT distinguishes itself from both Calvinism and Arminianism. Both traditions either implicitly or explicitly make doing good works a condition of salvation. At best, they diminish the gospel. At worse, they preach a different gospel.

I will leave it to you to decide where Wayne Grudem stands.

---

[4] *Free Grace Theology: 5 Ways It Magnifies the Gospel*, ed. Grant Hawley (Allen, TX: Bold Grace Ministries, 2016); Anthony B. Badger, *Free Grace Theology on Trial: A Refutation of "Historical Protestant" Soteriology* (N.P., N.D., 2017); *A Defense of Free Grace Theology: With Respect to Saving Faith, Perseverance, and Assurance*, ed. Fred Chay (The Woodlands, TX: Grace Theology Press, 2017).

CHAPTER 1

Inconsistent with Historic Protestantism?

THIS CHAPTER IS off topic. As Hillary Clinton famously said, "What difference does it make?"

Even if FGT is inconsistent with the view of most Protestants on what one must do to be saved, that would not prove anything. Is historic Protestantism the standard for determining what is, or is not, the gospel?

As Oliver Crisp says, the "confessions of the past... are theological guides. However, they too must be subjected to the Word of God anew each generation... Sometimes they will be found wanting. So it seems that there is reason to think that the reforming task is an ongoing one."[1]

What matters is what the Word says, not what the Reformers said.[2]

In addition, what Grudem actually says is ineffective in proving that the Reformers agreed with him.

---

[1] Oliver D. Crisp, *Saving Calvinism: Expanding the Reformed Tradition* (Downers Grove, IL: IVP Academic, 2016), 44.
[2] I should also add that many people who hold to FGT do not identify with historic Protestantism in the first place. Instead, they come from Baptist, Plymouth Brethren, and independent Bible churches, not from mainline Protestantism.

Grudem's first point in Chapter 1 is that Protestants since the Reformation have taught that truly born again people will persevere in faith and good works until death. He tries to support this view by quotes from people from the 16th to the 20th century, yet the quotes fail to prove his point.

He opens with two quotes from Calvin, which simply suggests that all who are born again will produce *some good works*. Neither quote defends perseverance.

The Formula of Concord (1576), the Thirty-Nine Articles of the Church of England (1571), the Westminster Confession (1646), and the New Hampshire Baptist Confession (1833) are cited next. Once again, the quotes do not discuss the perseverance of the saints. They merely say that born again people will produce acts of charity and hope.

His final citations from Wesley (1703-1791) and the Assembly of God Statement of Fundamental Truths (1916) again link regeneration and works, but fail to discuss the issue of perseverance.

FGT teaches that regeneration does result in some good works in all who live some length of time after the new birth. (Obviously if someone died at the very moment of the new birth there would be no time for any good works to be done.) Indeed, I would go so far as to say that there has not been a single *unbeliever* who ever lived who failed to produce some good works (Isa 64:6; Acts 10:35). The righteous deeds of unbelievers like Cornelius (Acts 10:1-8; cf. 11:14) have no *merit* with God—they are like filthy rags before God, who is perfect—but they are still good works. Why? Because even the unregenerate still have the image of God within them. It was marred by the Fall of Adam and Eve, but the image of God was not destroyed.

Grudem showed too little with his citations. He could have found many quotes, especially from modern Calvinists, who say that all who are truly born again will persevere in faith and good works until death. But he did not.

Even if we were to grant Grudem's argument that all the Reformers taught the regenerate persevere in faith and good works until death, that still does not establish that justification by faith alone, apart from works, is a doctrine that diminishes the gospel.

Moreover, Grudem fails to show that a single Reformer said that one needs *heartfelt trust* in Christ to be born again. Nor does he show a single Reformer who said that one must submit to the Lordship of Christ to be born again. Nor were any quotes given about the need for a *personal encounter* with Christ.

Grudem's second point is a non-sequitur. That is, it doesn't follow from what he showed under his first point. His second point is: "Therefore, the Free Grace movement today is not upholding the Reformation doctrine of *sola fide*, or 'justification by faith alone'" (p. 32).

But the quotes he gave do not show that.

In addition, Grudem fails to cite even one Free Grace person who says anything that contradicts what he had just quoted. If he wishes to make a claim like this, then he needs to cite Free Grace writers or speakers and show how they contradict justification by faith alone.

Illustrations can help clarify what an author means. Grudem gives us an illustration of a key ring with four different keys on it (p. 37). According to Grudem, the blue key opens his office door, but that the blue key is never found by itself, and is never alone from the other three keys. His point is that saving faith is likewise, never found by itself. It is always accompanied by other things like repentance and good works.

I do not think the illustration is very successful.

The blue key is never alone?

Surely the four keys were each cut separately and then put on his key ring. So they were alone at the start.

In addition, his illustration fails since the blue key works if detached from the ring. I have many keys on my key ring and I sometimes take one off and I find it always works just as well alone as it did with the other keys nearby.

Is faith already attached to good works at the moment of the new birth? If so, that would mean that good works are a necessary precursor to the new birth. If not, then at the moment one is born again faith is indeed alone, apart from works.

Maybe Grudem believes that at the exact moment of the new birth a number of good works spontaneously occur. If so, he does not say this or try to prove it from Scripture. Even so, these good works would still follow faith, even if only by a nanosecond.

Grudem admits that born again people sin and that the works of believers are not always exemplary. In Grudem's view, believers might go days or weeks or months or years without having a life that is characterized by good works. But how can that be if his illustration is correct and the key is never found by itself? If a believer had even one minute where an abundance of good works were not joined with his faith, then his faith would be proven false, and he would be proven unregenerate because saving faith is never alone.

Maybe what Grudem means is that good works are joined with saving faith *much of the time.* Of course, that does not fit his illustration which says faith is *never* found by itself. But even if that is what he means, then how much time can occur without a life overflowing with evident good works before the person should conclude he is not really born again? Grudem will address this question in the third chapter, but the answer is far from reassuring.

Grudem's final point in Chapter 1 is that justification by faith alone is an important doctrine.

No argument there.

He concludes the chapter by saying that the real question is what the New Testament teaches about the essence of saving faith. Agreed. But, as we shall see in Chapter 4, his view of saving faith is not found in the New Testament at all.

Improperly Preaching Repentance?

I WROTE MY doctoral dissertation at Dallas Seminary (1985) on repentance and salvation.[1]

Thirteen years later I changed my view of repentance.[2]

In reading what Grudem writes, it does not appear that he has given this as much thought as he ought. His discussion of New Testament texts that speak of repentance reflects an inadequate attention to the contexts.

In fact, in most cases *he does not discuss the texts at all*! He simply quotes them and moves on.

Repentance in Summaries of the Gospel

Grudem's first point in Chapter 2 is that, "Repentance from sin [is] in many summaries of the gospel" (p. 41).

---

[1] Robert N. Wilkin, *Repentance as a Condition for Salvation in the New Testament*, Unpublished doctoral dissertation, Dallas Theological Seminary, 1985. Six articles in *Journal of the Grace Evangelical Society* summarize my findings and can be found at faithalone.org/journal.
[2] Robert N. Wilkin, "Does Your Mind Need Changing? Repentance Reconsidered," *JOTGES* (Spring 1998): 35-46.

What would you do if you wanted to prove that? You would go to passages that you think deal with what one must do to be born again—if that is what you mean by "the gospel"—which Grudem does. Then you would show the reader that the passages indeed concern the new birth, and not something else. And you would show that repentance is mentioned as a condition of everlasting life in some or many of these "summaries of the gospel."

Grudem did not do any of that.

He did not establish that a single passage he cites is evangelistic, i.e., that it explains what one must do to be saved.

Not one.

HEBREWS 6:1

His first passage is Heb 6:1. Is that a gospel summary?

No.

This verse is written to born-again people (Heb 6:4-5). The mention of "repentance from dead works" concerns the works of the Mosaic Law. The believing Jewish readers were being challenged by false teachers to return to animal sacrifices for their salvation from eternal condemnation. The works of the Law are dead works. The readers had to turn from those works as part of the foundation of their Christian experience. They needed to be reminded of that truth.

Hebrews 6:1 has nothing to do with what one must do to be born again.[3]

---

[3] See J. Paul Tanner, "Hebrews," in *The Grace New Testament Commentary* (Denton, TX: Grace Evangelical Society, 2010), 1051-56; Zane C. Hodges, "Hebrews," in *The Bible Knowledge Commentary*, New Testa-

LUKE 24:47

Grudem's second proof text is Luke 24:47, the Great Commission passage in Luke.

As in the Great Commission in Matt 28:18-20, where baptizing and discipleship are said to be the work of the disciples, the Lucan passage concerns more than evangelism.

Grudem says, "This is Jesus's summary, after his resurrection, of the gospel message that his disciples would proclaim throughout the world" (p. 43). But that is an imposition on the text. Where is the call to believe? Does Grudem think that faith in Christ does not need to be in the Lord's summary of the gospel? Where is the promise of everlasting life? Again, it is not in the Lord's summary according to the author.

Grudem makes a claim that is not supported by the text. Simply claiming that this is an evangelistic text is a far cry from showing that it is.

Charles R. Erdman's comment on Luke 24:44-49 is helpful:

> The Scriptures [vv 44-45: the Law, the prophets, the Psalms] contain authoritative messages concerning Christ; these messages can be understood only by those who believe in Christ and are guided by him; the essential truths concerning Christ center in the facts of his death and resurrection [v 46]; *in virtue of the salvation thus secured, repentance and*

---

ment Edition (NP: Victor Books, 1983), 792-97.

forgiveness of sins can be preached... (emphasis added).[4]

ACTS 2:38

The Church of Christ's favorite verse is Acts 2:38. They use it to support their idea that there are five conditions of everlasting life: believe; obey; confess; repent; and be baptized. In their view, Acts 2:38 teaches no one can be born again apart from baptism and that lifelong ongoing repentance (as well as confession, belief, and obedience) is needed to retain everlasting life, since in their view it can be lost. This verse supposedly has the last two of those five conditions.

It amazes me that Grudem would use Acts 2:38 as his third proof text. He gives no discussion of the text other than to note that "faith is not even named in this verse," which is a major problem for *his* view, too, since he believes faith is the condition for salvation. However, there is no explanation given.

Understood in context, it is clear that the listeners believed *before* they asked, "What shall we do?" (Acts 2:37).[5]

Note that earlier in Acts 2:37 Luke says, "Now when they heard this, they were cut to the heart..." What they had just heard is that when they crucified Jesus they crucified "both Lord and Christ [Messiah]." They believed in Jesus at that point, but they wanted to know what they should do since they now realized that they

---

[4] Charles R. Erdman, *The Gospel of Luke* (Philadelphia, PA: The Westminster Press, 1966), 256.

[5] See Zane C. Hodges, *Harmony with God: A Fresh Look at Repentance* (Dallas, TX: Redención Viva, 2001), 102.

had taken part in killing the Messiah. Peter told them that in order to receive the Holy Spirit and receive the [fellowship] forgiveness of sins, they had to repent and be baptized.

The issue here is discipleship, not justification.

Lanny Thomas Tanton, a former Church of Christ minister, later went to Dallas Theological Seminary and wrote his master's thesis on Acts 2:38. He shows that in Acts the reception of the Spirit and the forgiveness of sins often occurred *after the new birth*.[6]

Grudem focuses on the word *repent*, but ignores the conjoined command to be baptized. That is more than an exegetical lapse. It is reading his theology into the text and ignoring anything that contradicts his position.

Are we to understand from Grudem that baptism is a condition of everlasting life? If not, why not?

ACTS 3:19; 5:31

Next up are Acts 3:19 and 5:31. These are corporate re-offers of the kingdom to national Israel, not calls for individuals to be born again. Amazingly, Grudem gives no explanation at all.

ACTS 11:18

Then Grudem cites Acts 11:18 and gives a half-hearted effort at explanation. He says that "repentance that leads to life" means "repentance that leads to everlasting life." But even if Peter's companions meant that "repentance leads to *everlasting* life" as Grudem

---

[6] For a journal article in which he laid out his view of Acts 2:38, see Lanny Thomas Tanton, "The Gospel and Water Baptism: A Study of Acts 2:38," *JOTGES* (Spring 1990): 27-52. It is available online at https://faithalone.org/journal/1990i/Acts2-38.html.

suggests, that does not make it a condition. Prayer, church attendance, and Bible study lead to everlasting life, too, but they are not conditions of the new birth.

Most likely, Peter's companions meant that repentance leads to extended *physical* life. Repentance is routinely linked to physical life (Luke 13:3, 5; 2 Pet 3:9). This comment by Zane Hodges is on the mark:

> Secondly, if we thought that the reference in Acts 11:18 *was* a reference to *eternal* life, then we are left with a surprising and implausible idea in this context. We must infer in that case that the Jerusalem Christians just now realized that Gentiles could be eternally *saved*! But this is so unlikely as to be almost fantastic (emphases his).[7]

Grudem fails to mention that when Peter summarizes what happened when he evangelized Cornelius and his household, Peter says nothing about repentance. He only mentions *believing* in Acts 15:7-11 at the Jerusalem Council. And if Grudem were to look at what Peter said in Acts 10:43, he spoke of *believing in Jesus*, not repentance.

ACTS 17:30-31

In his message in Athens at the agora, the Apostle Paul famously said, "Truly, these times of ignorance God overlooked, but now commands all men everywhere to repent, because He has appointed a day on which He will judge the world in righteousness by the Man whom He

---

[7] Hodges, *Harmony with God*, 117. His entire discussion (pp. 117-19) is worth examining.

has ordained. He has given us assurance of this to all by raising Him from the dead" (Acts 17:30-31). Grudem lists this as one of the places in which "Paul's evangelistic preaching regularly includes a call to repentance" (p. 44). Grudem adds, "Paul is speaking here about repentance from one's sins, not merely a change of opinion or a change of mind, because the second half of the sentence warns of a final judgment 'in righteousness'" (p. 44).

Grudem cites Acts 17:30-31 because he feels it supports his view that the condition of everlasting life is more than faith in Christ. He thinks turning from sins is another condition.

However, not only is it impossible that regeneration is by faith alone and it is also by faith plus repentance, but the context of Acts 17:22-31 fails to mention what Grudem says every evangelist must mention. There is no call to faith in Christ, or what Grudem calls "a personal encounter with Christ" in these verses. If this is meant to be an example of Paul's evangelistic ministry, rather than an example of his pre-evangelistic ministry, why is there no mention of the cross of Christ, faith in Christ, or the promise of everlasting life? In fact, why is there no mention even of the name of Jesus in his address? (Paul did, however, mention Jesus' name in private conversations before he began his address, as Acts 17:18 shows.)

Remember Paul's audience. These were pagans who had never heard a word about Jesus, about the cross, about Jesus' (or any) resurrection, and likely they knew nothing of the Hebrew Scriptures. His audience was like a tribal group today that knows absolutely nothing about Christianity.

Paul's aim in this short message is to gain interest. Hopefully some of those listening would be intrigued and would want to learn more. Based on what Luke said at the end of this account, it is clear that is what happened.

Luke tells us in v 34 that "some men joined him and believed..." Luke expects the reader to know that these people believed *in Jesus for everlasting life.* But since he is writing to a believer, Theophilus, he does not spell that out. The wording of v 34 ("some men joined him and believed") suggests that they came to faith in Christ after they joined Paul, that is, after his speech on Mars Hill. Luke does not say, "some men believed and joined him..."

Paul mentions repentance and coming judgment in order to gain the interest of the audience. Paul wanted to bring his listeners to faith in Christ. But he also wanted them to repent. Even unbelievers benefitted from repenting. In the first place, they escaped heightened temporal judgment (e.g., Nineveh). In the second place, they became more open to Jesus' promise of life.

Final judgment is mentioned presumably because the Lord Jesus Christ promised that whoever believes in Him "shall not come into judgment" concerning everlasting life (John 5:24). Only unbelievers from this age will have their works judged at the Great White Throne Judgment (Rev 20:11-15). Paul surely followed up on this point when some of his listeners joined him to learn more.

The fact that Grudem does not interact with the context of Acts 17:30-31 at all anywhere in his book is telling.[8] He is using those verses as proof texts and nothing more.

ACTS 20:21

Paul was in Miletus with Luke, on his way to Jerusalem. While there he sent a message to Ephesus and asked the elders to come so that he might speak to them. Acts 20:21 is part of what he said. He says concerning his ministry in Ephesus, "…I taught you publicly and from house to house, testifying to Jews, and also to Greeks, repentance toward God and faith toward our Lord Jesus Christ."

Grudem believes that Paul is here "summarizing his gospel message to the city of Ephesus" (p. 44). He suggests that *repentance toward God* "means it must be a repentance that involves personally turning *toward* him and coming into his presence" (p. 45).

There are multiple problems with what Grudem says about Acts 20:21.

---

[8] His longest discussion is found on part of pp. 126-27. Amazingly there he says, "the one and only thing [Paul] says that God commands is that they repent. In such a context, this wording cannot be anything other than the heart of his gospel message. The call to repent is best understood as Paul's explanation of the only way to escape the judgment that he warns of in the second half of the same sentence." Is Paul contradicting the Lord Jesus? The Lord said the only way to escape final judgment was to believe in Him (John 5:24). Is Paul contradicting himself? In the previous chapter of Acts, when asked, "What must I do to be saved?" Paul's answer was, "Believe on the Lord Jesus Christ and you shall be saved." He did not mention repentance there. What about in Galatians where Paul explains and defends his gospel. He mentions believing (3xs) or faith (21xs) twenty-four times in Galatians. Yet Paul does not mention repentance at all in Galatians.

First, he does not discuss "faith in our Lord Jesus Christ." That is bad exegesis. Faith in our Lord Jesus Christ is Paul's evangelistic message. That is clear from Romans, Galatians, Ephesians, and the book of Acts.

Second, Grudem does not explain the connection between "repentance toward God" and "faith in our Lord Jesus Christ." Some think Paul called Jews to faith in the Lord Jesus Christ and that he called Gentiles to repentance toward God. However, that does not fit the book of Acts. Paul called for both Jews and Gentiles to believe in the Lord Jesus. And he called all men, both Jews and Gentiles, to repentance toward God. The question is, how do these two different summaries fit together? Grudem does not say.[9]

Third, Grudem fails to explain why this is a summary of Paul's "gospel ministry." If by *gospel ministry* Grudem means that as shorthand for all of Paul's ministry, evangelism and discipleship, then he is correct.

---

[9] He does have a footnote, note 4 on page 45, in which he cites Dan Wallace as saying that there is "some sort of unity" between repentance (*metanoia*) and faith (*pistis*). Grudem does not explain what Wallace means. When we go to Wallace, *Greek Grammar Beyond the Basics*, p. 289, we see that Wallace thinks that Granville Sharp's rule applies here. However, Sharp's rule only applies to two personal nouns connected by *kai* in which only the first noun has the definite article. In such cases the two nouns *refer to the same person*. For example, Titus 2:13 refers to "the great God and our Savior Jesus Christ." There God and Savior refer to the same person, Jesus. But repentance and faith are not people. They are not personal nouns. Wallace says that in Acts "saving faith *includes* repentance" (italics his). Wallace goes on, "In those texts which speak simply of faith, a 'theological shorthand' seems to be employed: Luke envisions repentance as the inceptive act of which the entirety may be called *pistis*." That does not make sense. It does not fit the contexts in Acts. It clearly does not fit Acts 20:21. Wallace is expressing his theological bias there, not discussing Greek grammar. In any case, none of that is mentioned by Grudem.

That is what Paul is doing here, summarizing his entire ministry.

But if Grudem means, and he does, that Paul is summarizing specifically his evangelistic ministry, then that does not at all fit the particulars of the book of Acts. In Acts 15 at the Jerusalem Council Paul's evangelistic ministry is on trial. The conclusion of the Council is that the only condition for Gentiles to be born again, as for Jews, is faith in Christ (Acts 15:7-11). In Acts 16:31, in answer to the specific question, "What must I do to be saved?" Paul answered, "Believe on the Lord Jesus Christ and you shall be saved."

Nor does Grudem's explanation of Acts 20:21 fit with the book of Ephesians. Paul was speaking to the Ephesian elders. In the letter to the Ephesians Paul reminded them that salvation, everlasting life, is by grace through faith and apart from works (Eph 2:8-9). The words *repent* and *repentance* do not occur even once in the letter to the Ephesians. Yet the words *faith* (8xs) and *believe* (2xs) occur ten times.

Fourth, if Paul preached that repentance is a co-condition with faith for everlasting life, then he contradicted the Lord Jesus Christ (John 3:16-18; 5:24; 6:35), John the Baptist (John 3:36), Peter (Acts 10:43; 15:7-11), the Apostle John (1 John 5:1, 9-13; Rev 22:17), and he himself (Acts 16:31; Rom 4:4-5; Gal 2:15; 3:6-14; Eph 2:8-9).

ACTS 26:19-20

Grudem is picking out every time that Paul mentions repentance where the context might be construed as evangelistic. In Acts 26:19-20, Paul is sharing his testimony before King Agrippa. He has just told how he met and spoke with the resurrected Lord Jesus Christ on the road to Damascus (Acts 26:12-18). In that meeting Paul not only came to faith in Christ, but he was given a commission by him.

In vv 19 and 20 Paul is indicating that he has thus far been faithful to the commission the Lord Jesus gave him. He told Agrippa, "I...declared first to those in Damascus and in Jerusalem, and throughout all the region of Judea, and then to the Gentiles, that they should repent, turn to God, and do works befitting repentance." Grudem says,

> This summary of Paul's gospel presentation includes both repentance and turning to God, but again, faith is not even named explicitly. Paul's mention of "performing deeds in keeping with their repentance" indicates that a changed pattern of life is expected to follow, and that implies once again repentance *from one's sins,* not merely a change of mind about certain theological matters, is in view" (p. 46).

Grudem later cites Acts 26:19-20 and says that Paul "summarize[d] to King Agrippa...his gospel message" (p. 69).

I thought maybe I missed it, so I did a concordance study for *gospel message* and *gospel* in Acts 26. Did Paul say that he was summarizing his gospel message? No. The word *gospel* is not found in Acts 26. Indeed, the last use in Acts is Acts 20:24. The expression *gospel message* does not occur in Acts.

The word *gospel* occurs six times in Acts. When we look at these six uses (Acts 8:25; 14:7, 21; 15:7; 16:10; and 20:24), we do not find a single place which discusses repentance. In Acts 8:25 Philip preached the gospel in many villages of the Samaritans. Based on his ministry earlier in Acts 8, it is clear that Philip called people to faith in Christ, not to repentance (Acts 8:12-13, 32-39). In Acts 14:7 Paul and Barnabas were preaching the gospel in Lystra and Derbe. The preceding context in Pisidian Antioch suggests that they were calling people to faith in Christ (Acts 13:46, 48). In Acts 15:7 Peter says, "God chose among us, that by my mouth the Gentiles should hear the word of the gospel and believe." No mention of repentance. Again. In Acts 16:10, Paul indicates that because of the Macedonian vision they concluded "the Lord had called us to preach the gospel to them." Acts 16:31 shows that the message Paul preached was calling for believing on the Lord Jesus Christ. Repentance is not mentioned. In Acts 20:24, Paul speaks to the Ephesian elders of the ministry the Lord gave him, "to testify to the gospel of the grace of God." While earlier in the chapter he mentions both "repentance toward God" and "faith toward our Lord Jesus Christ" (Acts 20:21, see discussion above), the other five uses of *gospel* in Acts show that *faith toward our Lord Jesus Christ* is the gospel message mentioned in Acts 20:24.

None of this is mentioned by Grudem. That is strange. If we want to learn about Paul's gospel preaching, wouldn't we look up the uses of the word *gospel* in Acts?

I speak all over the United States and occasionally in other countries. All of my messages fall into two main categories: evangelistic and discipleship. By *evangelistic messages* I mean messages in which I am either seeking to lead unbelievers to faith in Christ, or messages in

which I am seeking to clarify or defend the promise
of life to believers. By *discipleship messages* I mean
any messages in which I am calling for believers or
unbelievers to follow Christ.

Now if I said that I preach everywhere to Jews
and to the Gentiles "that they should repent...and do
works befitting repentance," then I'd be talking about
my discipleship ministry. If I said that I preached
concerning faith in Christ (Acts 24:24; Rom 3:22; Gal
2:16; 3:14, 22, 26; Phil 3:9), then I'd be talking about my
evangelistic ministry.

How does Grudem explain *doing works befitting
repentance* as being part of Paul's *evangelistic message*? As
cited above, he says that this "indicates that a changed
pattern of life is expected to follow" (p. 46). But how
could that be? If Paul is stating what one must do to
have everlasting life, which is what Grudem says, then
producing good works would not merely be what is
"expected to follow." No. Good works would be one of
the conditions of everlasting life. If the good works did
not follow, the person would be eternally condemned.
Grudem favorably cites Tom Schreiner as saying, "good
works are necessary for eternal life" (p. 139).

That is no isolated statement. Grudem actually says
repeatedly in *Five Ways* that "the faith that justifies is
never alone" (pp. 28, 29, 30, 33, 36, 38, 71, 106, 110, 135,
139, 141, 146). For example, he says that

> the faith that justifies is never alone because
> it never occurs by itself, but is always
> accompanied by—or includes[10]—repentance

---

[10] Note the word *includes*. Grudem here says that "the faith that justifies...
includes repentance from sin" and that it is always followed by "doing

from sin and is always followed by other actions such as doing good works and continuing to believe" (p. 38).

Grudem also says that "saving faith results in obedience and faith results in perseverance" (p. 74).

It is likely that "turning to God" in Acts 26:20 refers to faith in Christ. Two verses earlier in Acts 26:18 the expressions *turning to light* and *turning to God* are said to be by faith in Christ. See also Acts 14:15 where turning to God appears to refer to turning to Him in faith. If that is correct, then Paul is once again summarizing his entire ministry, discipleship and evangelism. Repentance and works befitting repentance are part of his discipleship ministry. Turning to God would be a summary of his evangelistic ministry. If turning to God is a synonym for repentance, which seems unlikely in 26:20 and elsewhere in Acts, then this would simply be a reference to Paul's discipleship ministry.

2 PETER 3:9

Grudem quotes 2 Pet 3:9 and says, "For unbelievers to be saved, Peter says that it is necessary that they should 'reach repentance'" (p. 47). This understanding of 2 Pet 3:9, though common, does not fit the passage. At all.

In order to understand this verse, you need to understand 2 Pet 3:1-8 and 2 Pet 3:10-12. Both concern the Second Coming of Christ and the judgments associated with that coming.

In v 6 Peter reflects on Noah's flood. Peter says that the world that existed at the time of Noah "perished, being flooded with water."

Clearly the *perishing* mentioned in v 6 is not eternal condemnation. Peter is speaking of physical death, not eternal condemnation.

Grudem assumes, as I once did, that *apollumi* in 2 Pet 3:9 refers to eternal condemnation. But it refers to physical death in v 6. And that means it is highly possible that it also refers to physical death in v 9, just three verses later.

If v 9 refers to physical death as well, then the point Peter is making is not about heaven and hell, but about life and death.

That v 9 is talking about the deadly consequences of not repenting as compared with the life-extending benefits of repentance is supported by the repentance of the Ninevites in Jonah 3 (cf. Matt 12:41). Clearly God didn't wish for the Ninevites to perish, but for all of them to come to repentance. They did repent and thus Jonah's prophecy of death in forty days was averted.

2 Peter 3:9 is not an evangelistic verse. The context is not at all about evangelism. The context is about the Second Coming and temporal judgment.

Peter is saying that the reason God delays the Second Coming is that billions will die in the Tribulation and He doesn't want that. He doesn't want any to die prematurely. Since repentance is the cure for premature death, as long as the sins of mankind are not filled up, the Tribulation will not come. Repentance forestalls the Tribulation.

2 Peter 3:10-12 supports this understanding. Those verses look at the destruction of the current heavens and

earth after the Millennium. That is temporal judgment. God will eventually eliminate all traces of sin from the world and the universe.[11]

Indeed 2 Pet 3:9 refers to premature physical death (compare 2 Pet 3:6) as the consequence for not repenting.[12]

Grudem does not exegete a single passage. He just assumes his position and quotes some proof texts. That does not lead the reader to have confidence in his findings.

Repentance in Narrative Examples

Here, Grudem looks at examples from Jesus' ministry, presumably where Jesus called people to turn from their sins. However, he gives only three examples, spends only one page discussing them, and in none of the examples is repentance even mentioned!

Grudem seems to hold to works salvation based on the way he discusses all three examples.

The rich young ruler's problem, according to Grudem, is that he failed to sell all that he had (p. 47). If he had, then he would have been born again according to Grudem. Wouldn't that be buying your salvation? Grudem does not discuss that. He just quotes Luke 18:22

---

[11] For more discussion of 2 Pet 3:9 and its context, see Zane C. Hodges, *Second Peter: Shunning Error in Light of the Savior's Return* (Denton, TX: Grace Evangelical Society, 2015), 101-119.

[12] See Zane C. Hodges, "Repentance and the Day of the Lord," *Grace in Focus*, September-October 1999: 1, 3-4 (available at https://faithalone. org/magazine/y1999/99E1.html). See also Bob Wilkin, "Rethinking the New Testament Concept of Perishing," *JOTGES* (Autumn 2010): 1-24, esp. pp. 20-21.

with zero explanation. And he fails to notice that repentance isn't even mentioned there![13]

Then he quotes John 4:16-18 and Jesus' interaction with the woman at the well. He thinks Jesus was telling her she had to clean up her life to be born again. Yet there is no command to repent. Indeed, repentance is not mentioned! The reason Jesus revealed that she'd been married five times and was currently living in sin was because this would convince her that He is the Messiah. That is precisely what she later said in John 4:25-26, 29. The issue in John 4 is believing, not repenting.

Finally he cites Zacchaeus in Luke 19:8-9, again with no discussion! He fails to recognize that repentance is not mentioned there either. And the reason Zacchaeus became a child of Abraham that day is because he believed in Messiah, as Abraham did (Gen 15:6; Rom 4:1-5).

Charles Erdman says, "By his faith the publican of Jericho showed himself to be a true son of Abraham, the 'father of the faithful.' His trust in Christ secured for him that salvation which is offered to all, even to the lowest and most hopeless and despised."[14]

Similarly, Marvin Pate says, "Zacchaeus's confession of sin [was] prompted by his faith in Jesus" and that as a

---

[13] GotQuestions.org has an article on the rich young ruler. The unnamed author writes, "In His conversation with the rich young ruler, Christ did not teach that we are saved by the works of the Law. The Bible's message is that salvation is by grace through faith (Romans 3:20, 28; 4:6; Galatians 2:16; Ephesians 2:9; 2 Timothy 1:9). Rather, Jesus used the man's love of money to show how the man fell short of God's holy standard—as do we all. The rich young ruler needed the Savior, and so do we." See https://gotquestions.org/rich-young-ruler.html. Accessed November 30, 2016.

[14] Erdman, *The Gospel of Luke*, 194.

result of his faith "the Lord declared that salvation had come to the toll collector's house that day."[15] He goes so far as to suggest that "his seeking Jesus (v. 3) turned out to be the result of Jesus first seeking him (v. 10)."[16]

Repentance from Sin in Protestant Confessions

The author only cites the Westminster Confession and the Baptist Faith and Message. But whether he cites two or two hundred Protestant confessions, this proves nothing. Indeed, shouldn't this discussion be in Chapter 1, where he discusses Protestant theology?

Admittedly, turning from sins is considered a condition of everlasting life by the majority of Protestants. But consensus theology is often wrong.[17] As Oliver Crisp notes,

> The fact that the majority position on a given topic is one thing rather than another does not in and of itself make the majority right. Truth is not established by democracy; it is independent of the number of votes we give it. Indeed, the truth is sometimes held only by a tiny minority...[18]

---

[15] C. Marvin Pate, *Luke Commentary* (Chicago, IL: Moody Press, 1995), 353.

[16] Ibid., 354.

[17] See Stephen R. Lewis, "Consensus Theology Taints Biblical Theology," *JOTGES* (Autumn 2010): 27-41.

[18] Crisp, *Saving Calvinism*, 100.

Why Is Repentance Not Mentioned in John's Gospel?

I commend Grudem for admitting that repentance is not found in John's Gospel. Clearly this is a major problem for his view since John's Gospel is the only evangelistic book in the Bible (cf. John 20:30-31).[19]

Grudem has six explanations on how repentance can be a condition for the new birth and yet not be mentioned in John's Gospel. None of them is convincing.

First, he says that you can't base doctrine on only one book of Scripture. That is not true.

Of course you can!

All Scripture is God-breathed. That means every book is correct and we can learn doctrine from any book.[20] Surely Grudem is not saying that John's Gospel is contradicted by other books. Thus, this first point is patently false. Besides, repentance is not found in Galatians either. And Galatians is Paul's defense of his gospel. But Grudem fails to mention or discuss that. Indeed, James D. G. Dunn said that repentance "is a category strikingly absent from Paul."[21]

---

[19] See Zane C. Hodges, "Introducing John's Gospel: In the Upper Room with Jesus the Christ," *JOTGES* (Spring 2008): 29-44 and "Miraculous Signs and Literary Structure in John's Gospel," *JOTGES* (Autumn 2008):15-27.

[20] Only in 1 Corinthians 11 do we learn that women are to wear head coverings when praying or prophesying. However one understands that text, it is only found in one chapter of one book. But that does not mean we cannot understand and apply it. Though the Rapture is found in quite a few passages in Scripture, only 1 Thess 4:16-17 specifically and directly mentions the Rapture. The Rapture is true regardless of how few books of Scripture discuss it.

[21] James D. G. Dunn, "The Justice of God: A Renewed Perspective on Justification by Faith," *Journal of Theological Studies*, New Series, 43 (April 1992): 7.

Second, Grudem says that repentance is shown to be a condition of salvation in Jesus' teaching in Matthew, Mark, and Luke. To prove this he quotes four passages (again without any explanation): one in Mark, and three in Luke. None of them speak of everlasting life, salvation, or justification. None of them prove his point.

And why not quote any passages from Matthew? How can he prove that Matthew teaches this without at least citing passages from Matthew?

This is not careful study.

Besides, how does the fact that repentance is found in Jesus' teachings in the Synoptics prove that it is in the Fourth Gospel, when in fact it is not there?

Third, Grudem speculates that John was written late in the first century, long after the Synoptic Gospels. Grudem takes the position that John expected his readers to read the other Gospels along with his.

John was surely written before AD 70 (see John 5:2).[22] And it could have been the first Gospel written.

In addition, unlike the Synoptics which were written to believers, John said specifically that he wrote to unbelievers to lead them to faith in Christ and everlasting life (John 20:30-31).

That is a point that Grudem fails to discuss.

Anyone who has read John and the Synoptics recognizes that John's Gospel is far different and has a far different purpose. To suggest that John expected his unbelieving readers to find copies of other books that would supplement his book is a hard position to defend.

---

[22] See, for example, Leon Morris, *The Gospel According to John* (Grand Rapids, MI: Eerdmans, 1971), 34; Zane C. Hodges, *Faith in His Name: Listening to the Gospel of John* (Corinth, TX: Grace Evangelical Society, 2015), 95.

There is no evidence in John's Gospel for the need of companion books to help understand it.

Fourth, Grudem argues that Acts proves that repentance is a condition for everlasting life in John. Not only does Grudem not give any proof for this claim, he doesn't even quote a single proof text. No discussion and no proof texts equal a failure to defend one's view from Scripture.

How does he understand Paul's answer to the question, "What must I do to be saved?" in Acts 16:30? Why did Paul say, "Believe on the Lord Jesus Christ and you shall be saved…" (Acts 16:31), if Paul taught salvation as requiring repentance?

Grudem does not discuss that verse here or in the whole book. That is a serious oversight. Acts 16:30-31 contradicts his position.

Fifth, Grudem argues that in John's Gospel "we find several indications that he assumed repentance would be an essential part of what it means to believe in Jesus" (p. 52). That would mean that Jesus talked about repentance when he asked Martha, "Do you believe this?" That is reading into the text what Grudem thinks should be there, but is not.

So does John 3:16 really mean, "For God so loved the world that He gave His only begotten Son so that *whoever turns from his sins* shall not perish, but have everlasting life?"

The examples Grudem provides show that he adds to the Biblical definition of repentance.

Biblical repentance is turning from one's sin (Matt 12:39-41; compare Jonah 3:10). That is it.

Yet Grudem cites the following expressions in John as synonyms for repentance: the Holy Spirit *convicting people of sin* (John 16:8); the Lord Jesus telling the woman at the well to *call her husband* (John 4:16); people having *personal interaction with Jesus*; the Lord Jesus *calling people to believe in Him*; and the Lord's *calls to follow Him.* Yet not one of those things is repentance.[23]

Sixth, Grudem suggests that the fact that certain words like *repent* and *repentance* are not found in John's Gospel proves nothing. Is he right? If John is writing an evangelistic book telling people how to be born-again (and he is), then for him to leave out repentance proves that repentance is not a condition for everlasting life.

For example, say that George Will wrote a book entitled, *The Greatest Generals of World War 2.* He never once mentioned General George Patton. Would it not be obvious that he does not consider Patton one of the greatest generals of WW2?

In the same way, the fact that John never mentions repentance in his Gospel shows he did not consider it necessary in order to have everlasting life. That is an argument *about* silence, not merely an argument *from* silence.[24]

Two Different Free Grace Views of Repentance

Another major problem with Chapter 2 is that Grudem muddies the waters on what FGT says regarding repentance and everlasting life.

He says that there are two FGT views on repentance and salvation: 1) repentance is required, but it is merely

---

[23] See Robert N. Wilkin, *The Ten Most Misunderstood Words in the Bible* (Corinth, TX: Grace Evangelical Society, 2012), 107-126.

[24] See Hodges, *Harmony with God*, 5-11.

a change of mind; and 2) repentance is an optional resolve to turn from sin.[25]

However, there are actually three or four views of repentance and salvation within FGT.

In addition to the change of mind and the view that repentance is turning from sins but is not required to be born again, there are the views of Charlie Bing and Jody Dillow.

Grudem puts Bing under the change of mind view, but that is not quite correct. Bing makes it clear that in his view repentance is also a change of heart that involves "a person's inner change of...moral direction":

> But there may be a better [definition of Biblical repentance]. When we examine what is meant biblically by *mind* (*nous*) we find that it is sometimes used for the inner orientation and moral attitude. (cf. Rom 1:28; 7:23, 25; Eph 4:17, 23; Col 2:18). Thus the mind, biblically speaking, is not always the pure intellect. So the best translation of *metanoia* would be a *change of heart*. It refers to a person's inner change of attitude and moral direction. The Bible does not psychologically dissect the inner person, but leaves it at that (emphases his).[26]

---

[25] The way he explains the second view is misleading. We do not say that repentance is optional, any more than we say that church attendance or baptism are optional. Yes, a person can be born again without repenting, attending church, and being baptized. But if a person does not turn from his sins and follow Christ, he will be a miserable person in this life and he will suffer loss and shame at the Judgment Seat of Christ.

[26] Charlie Bing, *Grace Notes*, No. 22, 2016. Available online at http://www.gracelife.org/resources/gracenotes/ ?id=22. Last accessed Oct 19, 2016.

That is not quite the change of mind view that I advocated in my dissertation, or that was advocated by Lewis Sperry Chafer or Charles Ryrie.

Dillow goes a bit further. In his book *Final Destiny*, he suggests that, "repentance is a necessary precursor to saving faith."[27] He says that one must admit his sinfulness and guilt[28] and "must have a desire for moral change."[29] "There must be an acknowledgement of sin and a desire to be different."[30] "A nonbeliever must admit his sin to God, acknowledge he is wrong, and be willing to seek a new way of life."[31] That is not quite the change of mind view, either.

Grudem does discuss Bing's view of repentance and salvation, but only by quoting selectively from his dissertation. He misses Bing's discussion of repentance as a change of heart that includes an inner change of moral direction.

Though Grudem quotes from Dillow's *Final Destiny* in subsequent chapters, he does not discuss Dillow's view of repentance. That is odd, since Dillow's view is not only different, it is also closer to Grudem's view of repentance than any other view within FGT.[32]

Clearly, Grudem does not discuss all of the FGT views on repentance. Although he says all who hold to FGT reject the idea that one must regret his sins and reject the notion that one must desire to live a new life in

---

[27] Joseph C. Dillow, *Final Destiny* (NP: Grace Theology Press, 2013), 52.
[28] Ibid., 53-54.
[29] Ibid., 54, favorably quoting a missionary friend in Romania.
[30] Ibid.
[31] Ibid., 56.
[32] I do not think that the explanations of repentance by Bing and Dillow are consistent with FGT or with what they write elsewhere. However, if Grudem is discussing FGT on repentance, he should explain their views.

order to be born again, that is what Dillow says in *Final Destiny*. And Bing says something quite close to that in his dissertation and other writings.

The fact is, FGT holds multiple views on what repentance is and whether repentance is a condition for everlasting life. Chapter 2 of *5 Ways* fails to clearly delineate the views.

Saving Faith Does Not Include Obedience

Why is Grudem discussing saving faith and obedience in a chapter about repentance? Probably because he says that faith includes repentance and many people consider repentance to be a work.

Scripture calls repentance a work. For example, Jonah 3:10 says, "Then God saw *their works, that they turned from their evil way*; and God relented from the disaster that He had said He would bring upon them, and He did not do it" (emphasis added).

For some reason, Grudem is comfortable saying that saving faith *necessarily results* in a life characterized by good works (e.g., pp. 70-74), but he is not comfortable saying that saving faith *includes* obedience. According to the dictionary, the word *include* means "to contain." If saving faith is never without good works, then saving faith includes or contains obedience. Lack of obedience would prove lack of saving faith.

It should be noted that what Grudem denies toward the end of Chapter 2 (pp. 70-74)—that saving faith includes obedience—he inadvertently admits in Chapter 1.

Compare these two statements by Grudem in Chapter 1:

> The faith that justifies…is always *accompanied by—or includes*—repentance from sin and is always followed by other actions such as doing good works and continuing to believe (p. 38, emphasis added).

> …genuine faith *must be accompanied by good works*… (p. 33, emphasis his).

Grudem says that the words "accompanied by" mean "includes" (p. 38). Thus, when he says that "genuine faith must be *accompanied* by good works" he clearly means "genuine faith must *include* good works."

In this section, and later in the book when he discusses Jas 2:14-26, Grudem makes it clear that he believes that saving faith includes obedience. According to him, faith without works is not saving faith.

Grudem graduated from Westminster Theological Seminary and was influenced by the teachings of Dr. John Frame. Grudem actually endorses Frame's *Systematic Theology*. In that book, Frame says, "The second element of trust is subjection to Christ as Lord, a willingness to obey. As Jas 2:14-26 says, faith must be living faith, *obedient faith, faith that works*, or else it is dead" (emphasis added).[33]

In *5 Ways*, Grudem says the same things.

He says that heartfelt trust is an element of saving faith (Chapter 4), and that heartfelt trust is subjection to Christ as Lord (see esp. pp. 106, 110). Concerning Jas 2:14, Grudem says, "James begins this entire paragraph

---

[33] John Frame, *Systematic Theology* (Phillipsburg, NJ: P & R Publishing, 2013), 953.

by saying that faith without works cannot save someone" (p. 135). Grudem unambiguously says that faith without works cannot save anyone. In other words, Frame and Grudem are saying that it is *faith plus works which saves eternally.*

In this section, Grudem criticizes me for poor scholarship. Citing my book, *The Ten Most Misunderstood Words in the Bible,* he says:

> Robert Wilkin...says that those who disagree with Free Grace teachings say that "faith includes works," and that these people define faith as "including" obedience. But rather than documenting this claim by quoting from recognized theology texts and historic Protestant statements of faith (which never say that faith includes obedience), Wilkin simply attributes this view to unnamed "preachers and theologians" or to "radio and TV preachers, pastors, theologians, popular authors, and missionaries," or even to "most people within Christianity" (pp. 73-74).

Grudem makes a number of major errors here. They make me I wonder if he did more than skim a few pages of my book.

First, he errs by saying that I was talking about people who say *that faith includes works and obedience.* That is not what I was writing about. I was discussing people who say that "saving faith is different than regular faith," that "saving faith is not intellectual assent," that "saving faith is heart faith," that "saving faith is more than believing facts," that "saving faith is an ongoing commitment to obey," and that "saving faith always perseveres."[34]

Those are the headings.[35]

Why does Grudem say I am talking specifically about those who say that faith includes works? None of the headings in the chapter specifically address that issue.

Second, he errs by not quoting me. He just pulls out a few words or a phrase. The result is that he misleads the reader about what I was saying. And on one occasion he doesn't even get the phrase quite right. I wrote, "Most people from within Christianity…"[36] and he left out the word *from* indicating I said, "most people within Christianity." Worse than that minor mistake, he says I was talking there about people who say that faith includes works, when I was actually talking about people who "have rejected justification by faith alone apart from works."[37]

Third, he errs by criticizing me for not documenting others, even though I do. I mention by name and with full quotes—not just a word or phrase— Donald Dunkerly, John MacArthur, Gregory Koukl, James Danaher, Curtis Crenshaw, Alan Day, James

---

[34] Wilkin, *The Ten Most Misunderstood Words*, 8-15.

[35] Actually there are a few more headings in the chapter, but for the sake of space I left the final few off.

[36] In fact, I did not write that in my chapter on faith, which is where the other snippets he gives comes from. That snippet comes from the conclusion of the book, 160 pages later! So not only does he not give full quotes when he criticizes me for not giving quotes in my chapter on faith, he gives a misleading snippet from a different chapter.

[37] Ibid., 171. What I actually wrote was: "Most people from within Christianity today and over the centuries reject and have rejected justification by faith alone apart from works."

Montgomery Boice, and Darrell Bock.[38] True, I don't quote any denominational confessions. But to say I simply attributed these views to "unnamed" preachers and theologians is false. How could he miss seven pages of quotes? That is poor scholarship.

Grudem's Conclusion: A Weakened Gospel

Grudem writes, "My conclusion in this chapter is that the Free Grace movement preaches a weakened gospel because it avoids any call to people to repent of their sins" (p. 74).[39] Yet Grudem goes on to say that FGT is not a false gospel!

How can the message of FGT be the true gospel if it leaves out two elements that are central to what saving faith is, turning from sins and heartfelt trust that includes submission to the Lordship of Christ?[40]

Grudem cites the Free Grace Alliance covenant, which does not mention repentance, trust, or submission, and then says,

---

[38] Ibid, 8-14.

[39] Why would this make FGT "a weakened gospel?" Grudem does not explain, other than to say repentance "cannot be omitted without grave consequences in the lives of people who hear such a weakened message" (p. 74). But what if FGT does not *omit* repentance, per se, but simply says that it is not a condition of everlasting life? Would it still weaken the gospel?

[40] The false gospel anathematized by Paul in Gal 1:8-9 is the message that one is justified by works (Gal 5:4). Thus I would agree with Grudem that FGT is not a false gospel. However, his own message is very similar to that of the Judaizers. To be justified, Grudem says one must turn from his sins, submit his life to Christ, and follow Christ his entire life. That position is contradicted by Gal 2:16, as well as over 100 places in the New Testament where the sole condition of regeneration or justification is faith in Christ.

That statement is a wonderful summary of the New Testament gospel message, and it is inconceivable to me that anyone could read that statement and say that people who believe and advocate those truths are preaching a false gospel (p. 75).

But Grudem can't have it both ways.

If the summary of the New Testament gospel routinely includes *the need to turn from one's sins and to submit to the Lordship of Christ,* then leaving those things out must not be "a wonderful summary of the New Testament gospel message."[41]

If the FGA covenant is a fine statement, then Grudem just threw away his insistence that repentance must be preached in order to proclaim the New Testament gospel.

---

[41] Grudem does not interact with the GES affirmations of belief for some unknown reason. Since GES is the older organization, it would seem that any serious study of FGT would at least include a discussion of the GES affirmations and distinctives (e.g., assurance is of the essence of saving faith).

CHAPTER 3

Giving False Assurance?

Introduction

GRUDEM, LIKE MOST Evangelicals, does not believe
that it is healthy for people to be certain that they have
everlasting life. Such certainty, in his view, leads to
complacency and fewer good works.

Worse yet, such certainty actually keeps people
from being saved, as he argues in his first subheading of
Chapter 3 (see below).

The subheadings which follow in the next two
chapters are all Grudem's. We will consider the issues
as he lays them out, paying special attention to the
Scriptural support he cites.

The Result of the Weakened Free Grace Gospel Is Many Unsaved People

That heading suggests Arminianism, not Calvinism.
After all, according to Calvinism the elect will ultimately
be born again no matter what messages are preached
in various churches. The number of people who will

ultimately be saved never changes. But here Grudem says that "the weakened Free Grace gospel" results in "many unsaved people."

Grudem first presents an argument from experience. He says that people who hold to FGT

> wonder what is wrong with their Christian lives. Why do they not have the joy they see in Christians around them? Why does the Bible never seem to make much sense? Why is prayer not very meaningful? (p. 78).

We are not told who he has in mind. Is he writing about some of the people he cites in the book like Jody Dillow, Charlie Bing, Fred Chay, Dave Anderson, and Zane Hodges? I know those people and none of them to my knowledge wonder what is wrong with their Christian lives, why they have less joy than other believers, why the Bible doesn't make sense, or why their prayers are not meaningful.

This is a straw man argument.

Even if Grudem had provided examples, that would prove nothing.

I suppose if he could finance a random study of ten thousand Lordship Salvation folks and ten thousand Free Grace folks, then maybe he could draw some semi-scientific conclusions. But he did no study. He is just sharing his opinion.

He could be right. But then again, he could be wrong. Maybe it is Lordship Salvation people who typically lack joy, significance, and a meaningful prayer life?

Or maybe the vast majority of people in both groups do well on all counts.

What would any of this prove?

Nothing.

The issue is not who is happiest and most self-confident, but what the Scriptures teach.

Grudem gives no Scripture under this heading, which is inexplicable.

New Testament Epistles Frequently Warn Churchgoers That Some of Them Might Not Be Saved

The reader expects a discussion of a number of passages from the epistles where church people are warned they might not be saved. The author quotes from eight verses or short passages: Jas 2:14-17; 1 Cor 6:9-11; 2 Cor 13:5; Heb 3:12; 1 John 2:3-6; 1 John 3:6, 9-10, 14. *But Grudem does not explain any of these verses. He simply quotes them, assuming his proof texts need no explanation.*

Let's consider those eight passages Grudem quotes, but does not explain. When we do, we will see that none of them support his position.

JAMES 2:14-17

For further information about these verses, see the detailed discussion in Chapter 5.

What is evident, even at a cursory glance, is that James is addressing "my brothers" (2:14), not unbelievers, and that he is talking about a fellow "brother or sister" (2:15) who is in need. In light of Jas 2:1-13, verses not mentioned or discussed by Grudem even in Chapter 5, James is continuing the discussion of the way in which the readers were treating poor Christians inappropriately.

Verse 14 begins with the words which v 16 ends with: "What good is it?" (or, "What does it profit?"). James's point is that if a believer does not apply what he believes, then he will not be delivered from God's temporal judgment and his hungry and cold fellow believers will remain destitute. Faith without works is useless and unproductive. *Any time any believer fails to put his faith to work, his faith at that moment is not good. Faith without works is dead, that is, useless, unproductive, not good.*

To interpret Jas 2:14-17 to mean that faith without works is not faith does not fit logic, the context of Jas 2:1-13, the words used in 2:14-17, and the following context in Jas 2:18-26. That dog won't hunt.

1 Corinthians 6:9-11

Paul has three passages in his epistles which give a vice list and say that "those who do such things shall not inherit the kingdom of God." Those three texts are 1 Cor 6:9-11; Gal 5:19-21; and Eph 5:5-7. All three discuss not who will *enter the kingdom*, but who will *inherit the kingdom*.

When I was contemplating going on staff with Campus Crusade for Christ in 1974, my Dad told me that if I did he and Mom would disinherit me. I accepted that as the price I had to pay to pursue Christian ministry.

During the four years when I was on staff with CCC and presumably disinherited, my parents spoke with me on the phone, wrote me, and welcomed me to visit. I was still a member of the family, even though my inheritance was in doubt.

It turns out that Mom and Dad changed their minds and did not disinherit me after all. But that was a projected outcome. And it did not change my status as a member of the family.

Any believer who rebels against God and lives in the spiritual far country (Luke 15:11-32) is in danger of being disinherited by God. Paul said, "If we endure, we shall also reign with Him" (2 Tim 2:12a). But he also said, "If we deny Him, He will also deny us" (2 Tim 2:12b). That is, if we do not endure in our confession of Christ, then He will deny us the privilege of ruling with Him forever. Compare Matt 10:32-33. All believers will be with Him forever (1 Thess 5:10). But only faithful believers will rule with Him (1 Cor 4:1-5; 9:24-27; 2 Tim 4:6-8).

For more information on this important passage see the journal article I wrote about Gal 5:19-21, a parallel text.[1]

2 CORINTHIANS 13:5

As this verse is discussed in detail in Chapter 5, I will only briefly discuss it here.

First, Paul was defending his apostleship in 2 Corinthians and in this passage (cf. 2 Cor 10:12-17; 11:5, 13; 12:11-13; 13:1-10).

Second, the Greek of v 5 is emphatic: "*Yourselves* examine…" The word *yourselves* (*heautous*) is first in the Greek sentence. Why? Because they had been examining

---

[1] "Christians Who Lose Their Legacy: Galatians 5:21," *Journal of the Grace Evangelical Society* (Autumn 1991): 23-37.

not themselves, *but Paul*. Some were questioning Paul's apostolic authority. Did he really speak for God? Now he turns the tables. Do you really speak for God?

Third, the words "in the faith," "Jesus Christ in you," and "disqualified [lit. disapproved]" all refer in this context (and in other contexts in the New Testament) to the reader's experience, not to their position. Paul wants them to see if they are abiding in the faith, if Christ is at home in their lives, and if they are approved by Christ.

Fourth, the idea that Paul is here questioning whether the readers are born again is inconsistent with the immediate context and the entire letter. In both 1 and 2 Corinthians Paul affirms the regenerate status of the readers. He calls them *brethren*, a term he reserves in his letters for regenerate people, eight times in 2 Corinthians (2 Cor 1:8; 8:1, 23; 9:3, 5; 11:9, 26; 13:11), including once immediately after this passage (2 Cor 13:11). He calls them *brethren* an additional twenty-seven times in 1 Corinthians.

Paul speaks of the readers' faith in Christ three times in 1 Corinthians and five times in 2 Corinthians (1:24, "your faith...by faith you stand"; 4:13; 5:7; 8:7 "you abound...in faith"; 10:15, "your faith is increased").

Fifth, the issue here is *approval* or *disapproval*. In the three verses of 2 Cor 13:5-7 those words occur five times (*dokimazete, adokimoi* (x3), *dokimoi*). Compare 1 Cor 9:27 where Paul indicates that he himself might become disapproved (*adokimos*). Approval or disapproval are eternal rewards concepts, not eternal destiny concepts.

Paul is turning the tables on the readers and asking them to see if they are abiding in the faith, if Christ is at home in their lives, and if they are currently approved by Christ.

HEBREWS 3:12

It is easy to see that this verse is part of the second warning passage in Hebrews: "Beware, brethren, lest there be in any of you an evil heart of unbelief in departing from the living God, but exhort one another daily..." However, notice that the author calls them *brethren*.

Unbelievers are not brethren. Believers are brethren.

An unbeliever cannot depart from the living God because he has nothing to depart from. Only one with a relationship with the living God can depart from Him.

If our theology does not allow that a believer might depart from God and might develop "an evil heart of unbelief," then we need to change our theology. All five of the warning passages in Hebrews are warning born-again people of the danger of falling away from the faith. If they did fall away, they would experience terrifying temporal judgment from the living God (cf. Heb 10:31).

Of course unbelievers are not able to exhort believers daily. Believers are to exhort other believers as the Day approaches (cf. Heb 10:23-25).

Instead of being a text that proves Grudem's point that the New Testament epistles frequently warn churchgoers that some of them might not be regenerate, the opposite is the case. This verse affirms the regenerate status of the readers.

1 JOHN 2:3-6

One of the problems of proof-texting is that the author does not discuss the immediate context or the context of the entire book.

There are two major views on the purpose of
1 John. It either deals with various tests of whether one
has everlasting life or with tests of whether one is in
fellowship with God. The tests of everlasting life view
suggests that 1 John 5:13 is the purpose statement of the
book. The tests of fellowship view suggests that 1 John
1:3-4 is the purpose statement.

None of this is discussed by Grudem.

The evidence strongly supports 1 John 1:3-4 as the
purpose statement.

Epistles of that day normally put their purpose
statements, if there was one, at the start of the letter.
Compare Gal 1:6-10; Titus 1:5; Philem 8-11; Heb 1:1-4;
Jas 1:19-20; 1 Pet 1:3-12; 2 Pet 1:5-11; 3 John 4; Jude 3-4.

If the purpose of 1 John is to aid the readers in being
assured that they are in fellowship with God, then it is
easy to see how that is possible. They have assurance of
eternal destiny by faith alone (1 John 5:9-13).[2] Then if
they walk in the light and confess their sins they know
that they are walking in fellowship.

However, if the purpose of 1 John is to help the
readers determine if they are born again or not, then
1 John 5:9-13 no longer is seen as assurance by faith
alone. Instead, Grudem and others see those verses as
granting assurance to those who have *true faith*. And
what is *true faith*? True faith is found in your works,
Grudem says. The better your works, the more likely you
are to have true faith.

"How many good works does one have to do in
order to be assured of salvation?" Grudem asks (p. 92).

---

[2] Assurance of everlasting life is necessary to have assurance of fellowship
with God. One who is unsure whether he is a child of God necessarily
cannot be sure he is in fellowship with Him.

He answers, "Some. To be more specific, *some* change of life gives a basis for *some* measure of assurance" (p. 92, italics his). He then adds, "a greater change of life gives a basis for a stronger assurance" (p. 92).

Whatever *assurance* is for Grudem, it is not certainty. For him assurance is a measure of probability. A new professing believer has no changed life and hence zero probability that he will make it into Christ's kingdom. A professing believer who has some change has some small probability that he might make it. A professor with lots of change is more likely to make it.[3] But not certain.

If you do not have certainty of your eternal destiny by *faith alone*, you cannot have certainty.[4] No matter how much change of life a person has, he can never be certain based on his works because 1) he still sins (Rom 3:23); and 2) he can't be sure he will persevere in the future (1 Cor 9:27; 2 Tim 2:12).

1 John 1:5–2:2 gives tests to measure our fellowship with God. Starting in 1 John 2:3, the issue intensified to whether we know God intimately in our daily experience. A new believer is in fellowship with God (Acts 10:43). But he does not yet know God. He must grow to the point where he knows and keeps God's

---

[3] On p. 95 he responds to something I wrote. He attempts to restate this statement by me: "it is impossible to be sure of your eternal destiny." He thinks he is saying the same thing when he says "people...are unable to have *a confident assurance* of their own salvation" (emphasis added). I never spoke of confident assurance. That is Grudem's idea. That is the best he can hope for. He will go to his grave hoping that he really is a true believer. Well, unless, of course, he comes to see the truth of John 3:16; 5:24; 6:35; 11:25-27; Acts 16:31; Gal 2:16; 3:6-14; Eph 2:8-9; 1 Tim 1:16; and so forth. I pray that he does.

[4] Which is what assurance of eternal life really is. See Luke 10:20; John 11:25-27.

commands in order to know God in his experience. That
is the point of 1 John 2:3-11.

We know that we know Him in our experience if we
keep His commandments. Notice that 1 John 2:6 clarifies
this: "He who says *he abides in Him* ought himself also to
walk just as He walked." The issue is abiding in Christ, a
fellowship concept. See John 15:1-10.

Of course, since Grudem merely quotes these verses
and does not discuss them, he does not expound on the
concepts of abiding, knowing, and fellowship with God.

1 JOHN 3:6, 9-10

See the above discussion about the purpose of
1 John. That discussion is vital to understanding these
verses.

First John 3:6 concerns abiding in Christ. Grudem's
translation is in error. The Greek says nothing about
keeping on sinning. If it did, then no one would be
abiding in Christ since every single born again person
on earth keeps on sinning, as 1 John 1:8, 10 say. Indeed,
if we say we have no sin, we are liars and the truth is not
in us.

The Greek says, "Whoever abides in Him does not
sin. Whoever sins has neither seen Him nor known
Him." These are absolute statements. The point is the sin
is never an expression of seeing Him or knowing Him.

First John 3:9-10 continues that same point. Again, it
is absolute. The born-of-God part of us never sins. At the
core of our being believers are sinless. We sin because
the flesh intervenes. But that is not who we truly are.
John wants us to see ourselves as overcomers in Christ.

1 JOHN 3:14

The last verse Grudem quotes in this section is
1 John 3:14. The expression *passed from death to life*
is only found twice in the New Testament: John 5:24
and 1 John 3:14. Clearly, in John 5:24 it refers to one's
position. The believer has everlasting life (present tense),
shall not come into judgment (future tense), but has
passed from death to life (past tense).

Grudem merely quotes 1 John 3:14. He does not
explain it.

John Mitchell says, "This is experiential knowledge…
How can we know in our experience that we have eternal
life? It will be manifested in our love for the brethren."[5]

Zane Hodges says,

> The underlying implication is that the passage
> *from death to life*, which occurs at the point
> of salvation (John 5:24), can be experientially
> known and appreciated through Christian love.
> Since John wants his readers to 'have fellowship'
> with the apostolic circle (cf. 1:3), it is obvious he
> wants the readers to share the same experiential
> knowledge of the life they possess as children of
> God.[6]

In light of the purpose of 1 John (1:3-4), the point
in 1 John 3:14 is that we know we are *experiencing* God's
life when we love other Christians.

---

[5] John G. Mitchell, *Fellowship: A Devotional Study of the Epistles of John*
(Portland, OR: Multnomah, 1974), 99-100.

[6] Zane C. Hodges, *The Epistles of John: Walking in the Light of God's Love*
(Irving, TX: Grace Evangelical Society, 1999), 157, italics his. See also
Michael Eaton, *1, 2, 3 John & Jude* (Kent: Sovereign World Trust, 2011),
71.

Not one of the texts Grudem cites "warns churchgoers that they might not be saved," if by *saved* Grudem means regenerate, which he does. Surely he should have written a page or two about each of the eight texts to point out where a warning concerning eternal destiny is found. He should also discuss the Free Grace view of each text, but he says in a footnote that he will do that in Chap. 5. The funny thing is that of the eight texts he cites, he only discusses two in Chapter 5 (2 Cor 13:5; Jas 2:14-17). That is disappointing.

The Free Grace View Says That People Can Become Complete Unbelievers and Still Be Saved

That is our position. But Grudem does not show in this section why it is wrong for FGT to suggest that believers are eternally secure even if they later apostatize.

Grudem does not discuss the verses that clearly teach believers may apostatize.

Why no discussion of Luke 8:13, the second soil which "believes for a time and in time of temptation falls away?"

What about 1 Tim 1:18-20 and Hymenaeus and Alexander who "concerning the faith have suffered shipwreck?"

What about 2 Tim 2:16-19 and Hymenaeus and Philetus "who have strayed concerning the truth…and they overthrow the faith of some?"

We discuss all those texts and many more in our magazines, journals, books, and blogs.[7] But for some reason Grudem doesn't cite the texts we cite, or discuss

---

[7] For example, see my *Confident in Christ*, Chaps. 12 and 18.

them. If he is convinced that believers can't stop believing, then why not discuss key texts which say they can?

In this section Grudem keeps complaining that FGT does not ask people who profess faith in Christ to examine their works to see if they are born again. Yet those are people who profess faith, not people who do not, which is what this section of Chap. 3 is supposedly about.

Free Grace Teaching about Assurance Makes a Fundamental Category Mistake

Grudem, like other Lordship Salvationists, says, "The question is not 'How do I know that Christ has died for people's sins and that He will save all who believe in Him?'" He goes on, "The question is, rather 'How do I know *that I have truly believed?*'" (p. 85, italics his).

Grudem's supposed proof is once again quoting texts without a word of explanation. This time he cites six passages, three of which he quoted earlier, and three new ones. Without explanation, his quotes certainly do nothing to prove his point to those who are not yet convinced of his position. Once again, the passages he cites do not indicate that believers are being warned that they might end up in the lake of fire. Once again, Grudem does not present or discuss Free Grace interpretations of these texts.

Grudem's concern, which he brings to the Scriptures, and not which he finds in the Scriptures, deals with how one knows he has *truly believed.*

By putting the word *truly* before *believe*, Grudem changes "whoever believes in Him" in John 3:16 to "*whoever truly believes* in Him."[8] This allows Grudem to get in works, for saving faith involves works in his view.

Grudem fails to discuss the only place in the entire Bible where Jesus or any of the Apostles asked anyone if they believed in Him. That is John 11:26. After saying that He guarantees everlasting life to all who live and believe in Him, the Lord Jesus asked Martha, "Do you believe this?"

If Grudem was asked that question, he would answer by giving three lines of evidence that he *really believes this*: 1) the confidence he gets when he examines his works; 2) the good feeling the Holy Spirit gives him; and 3) the intellectual confidence he finds in the promises of Scripture to the *true believer*.

But how did Martha answer? Was she unsure whether she believed? Did she appeal to her behavior? No. Martha made the same alleged category mistake that FGT makes. She said, "Yes, Lord. I believe that You are the Christ, the Son of God who is to come into the world" (John 11:27).

No mention of works.

Or feelings.

Simply the mention of the Old Testament Scriptures which say that the Christ, the Son of God, was prophesied to come into the world and the evidence shows that Jesus is He.

Maybe in another edition of *5 Ways*, Grudem will explain Martha's response to the question, "Do you

---

[8] The idea that there is a sort of faith in Christ which will not save is contrary to what the Lord promised. As long as we believe in Him for what He promised, everlasting life, we are secure (John 3:14-18; 5:24; 6:35-47; 11:25-27). Speaking of *really believing* confuses people and strips them of assurance.

believe this?" and maybe he will explain the Lord's failure to question Martha about her works. The Lord seems guilty of giving Martha what Grudem calls "false assurance."

In this section Grudem answers the question, "How many good works does one have to do in order to be assured of salvation?" His answer is, "Some" (p. 92).

He continues, "To be more specific, *some* change of life gives a basis for *some* measure of assurance, and greater change of life gives a basis for a stronger assurance" (p. 92).

Herein lies the problem with Lordship Salvation: assurance is never certainty. It fluctuates based on one's works, one's feelings about one's works, one's sins, one's feelings about one's sins, etc. But Lordship assurance is not certainty because if greater change of life means stronger assurance, then the only way to have certainty would be to have a total change of life that never fluctuates, that is, glorification. Prior to death those following Grudem's type of theology will never be sure of their eternal destiny.

The Historic Protestant View Does Not Say That Assurance of Salvation Is Impossible, But Just the Opposite

Grudem is aware, of course, that his linkage of assurance with imperfect works and fluctuating feelings leads to the impossibility of certainty. So now he has a section supposedly showing that Lordship Salvation teaches that certainty of one's eternal salvation is possible.

He cites me as saying that under the Lordship Salvation view of saving faith "it is impossible to be sure of your eternal destiny..." and that "because no one's life is perfect, certainty of one's eternal destiny is impossible in this system" (p. 95).

He says that I misunderstand his position because in his view people can "have a confident assurance of their salvation in this lifetime" (p. 95).

Confident assurance is not *certainty*.

I spoke of *certainty now*. He spoke of *confidence in this lifetime*. There is a huge difference between the two.

You can be confident, but still have reservations. You can be confident, without knowing for sure. You can be confident, and still fear you are wrong. Confidence is not certainty.

However, Grudem then goes on and cites "the most influential Protestant tradition since the Reformation... the Westminster Confession of Faith" as saying that believers might attain "an infallible assurance" and might have "certainty" (p. 96).

Grudem misunderstands the Westminster Confession.

When it speaks of "an infallible assurance" and "certainty," it is talking about the Bible's promises. *Those promises are infallible and certain*, not the believer's subjective assurance.

Joel Beeke, a Reformed pastor and professor who wrote his doctoral dissertation at Westminster Seminary on Reformation and Post-Reformation theology, says:

> The Puritan composers of the WCF were consistent in reminding believers that the objective promise embraced by faith (never

apart from faith) is infallible because it is God's all-comprehensive and faithful covenant promise. Consequently, subjective evidence must always be based upon the promise and be regarded as secondary, for such is often mixed with human convictions and feelings even when it gazes upon the work of God. In fact, all exercises of saving faith apprehend, to some degree, the primary ground of divine promise in Christ.[9]

Thus the Confession pointed to one objective and infallible basis of assurance (the Word of God), and two subjective and fallible bases of assurance, (the inner witness of the Spirit and the works which the Spirit produces in and through us). But the Confession teaches that the objective promises alone will not produce assurance. One needs the promises *plus* the subjective bases of assurance.

Grudem does acknowledge that the WCF requires more than belief in the promises of God: "This assurance is based on several types of evidence as indicated by many New Testament passages" (p. 96). He indicated earlier in Chap. 3 that those evidences are "continuing in faith" (pp. 83-84)—that is, believing the objective promises of God, "seeing evidence in their good works" (p. 84), and "the inner testimony of the Holy Spirit" (p. 88).

Calvinist David Engelsma comments on the difference between the Puritan doctrine of assurance

---

[9] Joel Beeke, "Assurance of Faith: Promises, Inward Evidences, and the Spirit's Witness." See frcna.org/resources/student-society-speeches?download=20

(found in the WCF) and that of the Reformers:
"The Puritan doctrine of assurance was not that of
the Reformers. This is freely admitted by Reformed
theologians who defend the Puritan doctrine of
assurance."[10] He went on to say,

> For Calvin, all the Reformers, and the
> Reformation of the church in the sixteenth
> century, faith *is* assurance of salvation, faith
> *essentially* is assurance: "Faith is a firm and
> certain knowledge of God's benevolence toward
> us."[11]

Engelsma's concluding comments about the Puritan
view of assurance of salvation apply equally as well to
Grudem's view of assurance:

> Puritan preaching...is forever questioning your
> assurance, forever challenging your right to
> assurance, forever sending you on a quest for
> assurance, and forever instilling doubt. The
> Spirit does not work assurance by means of a
> gospel of doubt.[12]

Beeke, while lauding the Spirit's work in giving us *as
much assurance as possible*, inadvertently confirms what
Engelsma charges:

> For the divines of the Westminster assembly,
> all three grounds of 18.2—faith in God's
> promises, inward evidences of grace realized

---

[10] David Engelsma, *The Gift of Assurance* (South Holland, IL: The Evangelism Committee of the Protestant Reformed Church, 2009), 15.
[11] Ibid., 16, italics his.
[12] Ibid., 53.

through syllogisms, and the witness of the Spirit—must be pursued to obtain *as full a measure of assurance as possible* by the grace of God. If any of these grounds are unduly emphasized at the expense of others, the whole teaching of assurance becomes imbalanced or even dangerous. No Puritan of the stature of Westminster's assembly of divines would teach that assurance is obtainable by trusting in the promises alone, by inward evidences alone, or by the witness of the Holy Spirit alone.[13]

Not once does Grudem cite Calvinists who criticize the Puritan position on assurance. In addition to Engelsma, men like Kendall,[14] Zachman,[15] and Eaton[16] warn about the lack of certainty that prevails in Puritan theology.

Grudem is uncertain that he is born again because, by his own admission, his works and his feelings are subjective and fallible. Since he teaches that works plus feelings plus the promises of God are all needed to produce some measure of assurance, then the best he can have is what Beeke calls "as full a measure of assurance as possible." His position on assurance is what Engelsma labels "a gospel of doubt."

---

[13] Beeke, "Assurance of Faith," 10, italics added.

[14] R. T. Kendall, *Calvin and English Calvinism to 1649* (Eugene, OR: Wipf and Stock, 1997).

[15] Randall C. Zachman, *The Assurance of Faith: Conscience in the Theology of Martin Luther and John Calvin* (Minneapolis, MN: Fortress Press, 1993).

[16] Michael Eaton, *No Condemnation: A Theology of Assurance of Salvation* (Downers Grove, IL: InterVarsity Press, 1995).

Chapter 3 is entitled "False Assurance." While Grudem means that FGT offers false assurance, the truth is that the chapter title *applies to his own position*. Grudem, though well intentioned, promotes false assurance. That is, he promotes non-assurance.

What Grudem calls *assurance* is really *doubt*.

CHAPTER 4

Underemphasizing Trust in the Person of Christ?

Introduction

FAITH IN CHRIST, according to Grudem (and Lordship Salvation), is not believing in Him for the everlasting life He promises. Grudem calls that *mere intellectual assent*.

Grudem briefly discusses *mere intellectual assent* (one page), since in his view most in FGT do not hold to that position.

Instead, most Free Grace people, according to Grudem, believe that faith in Christ is both intellectual assent and trust in Christ (as evidenced by the five pages he devotes to this view). However, in his view the FGT view of trust in Christ is not robust enough.

Some Free Grace Advocates Say That Faith Equals Mere Intellectual Assent

The only people Grudem cites here are Zane Hodges, whom he calls "the founding father of the modern Free Grace movement" (p. 100), and me.

He cites Hodges as saying that "Faith…is an inward conviction that what God says to us in the gospel is true. That—and that alone—is saving faith" (p. 100).[1] He cites me as saying, "Stripped of its pejorative connotation, 'intellectual assent' is a good definition of what faith is" (p. 100).[2]

Hodges explained why he said that, but Grudem did not think it was important to give Hodges's evidence or interact with it. Hodges went on to quote and then discuss 1 John 5:9-13,[3] a passage which proves that faith is being convinced that a testimony is true. Hodges wrote,

> Since we often accept human testimony, how much more ought we to accept divine testimony? To do this is to possess that testimony inwardly—within ourselves. The opposite of this—unbelief—is to make God out to be a liar.[4]

Hodges ended his discussion of 1 John 5:9-13 by saying, "And when a person has God's word for it, they have no need to seek assurance elsewhere."[5]

It would be nice to see Grudem's response. But Grudem did not cite or discuss the support Hodges gave.[6]

---

[1] Zane C. Hodges, *Absolutely Free! A Biblical Reply to Lordship Salvation* (Grand Rapids, MI: Zondervan, 1989), 31.

[2] *Grace in Focus Magazine* (which Grudem wrongly identifies as "the Free Grace Journal," evidently not realizing that we have both a magazine and a journal), Sept-Oct 2014, 27.

[3] Hodges, *Absolutely Free*, 31-32.

[4] Ibid., 32.

[5] Ibid.

[6] Hodges gave much more support for his claim in the six and one half

In regards to Grudem's citation of me, it is odd that he picks an article in which I am summarizing, but not explaining or defending, FGT's view of saving faith. Elsewhere he cites my book, *The Ten Most Misunderstood Words in the Bible*.[7] I have an entire chapter in that book explaining and defending FGT's view of saving faith.[8] In an earlier book I have five chapters on saving faith.[9] It is a shame that he did not state my defense of my position.

Faith is intellectual assent of a proposition. As we shall see, Grudem's rejection of that view of faith is in reality an unintentional rejection of God's Word.

Other Free Grace Advocates Say That Faith Includes Trust in the Person of Christ

The discussion in this section is a bit confusing. At one point, Grudem quotes Hodges regarding faith being the conviction that facts or propositions are true. Yet he also says that Hodges taught that faith is trust in the Person of Christ. So is he suggesting that Hodges belongs in both category one and two?

Grudem also wonders whether Anderson and Dillow hold to faith as believing the promise of everlasting life or faith as trust in the Person of Christ.

---

pages that preceded that quote. Hodges quoted and discussed John 6:47; 20:30-31; Rev 22:17; Rom 10:14, 17. Yet Grudem does not tell us what he said about those passages and he does not respond to what he said.
[7] Robert N. Wilkin, *The Ten Most Misunderstood Words in the Bible* (Corinth, TX: Grace Evangelical Society, 2012).
[8] Ibid., 7-22.
[9] Robert N. Wilkin, *Confident in Christ*, 2nd ed. (Corinth, TX: Grace Evangelical Society, 1999, 2015), 17-56.

The idea that belief is always propositional rankles Grudem:

> Many wonderful Free Grace Christians whom I know *pray* to Jesus; they don't pray to propositions about Jesus. In church they *worship* Jesus; they don't worship propositions about Jesus (p. 102, italics his).

I wonder if Grudem has read Gordon Clark's famous book *Faith and Saving Faith*, in which he shows that all belief is propositional.[10] Clark was a Calvinist, but he recognized that the postmodern idea of faith being some sort of vague existential encounter (or feeling) is irrational.

In a section entitled, "Person or Proposition?" Clark, speaking about the type of argument that Grudem makes, writes:

> In spite of the popularity and supposedly superior spirituality of the contrast between a *mere* intellectual proposition and a *warm*, living person, it rests on a mistaken psychological analysis. Even Berkhof admits [p. 501], with at least an appearance of inconsistency, that "As a psychological phenomenon, faith in the religious sense does not differ from faith in general…Christian faith in the most comprehensive sense is man's persuasion of the truth of Scripture on the basis of the authority of God."

---

[10] Gordon H. Clark, *Faith and Saving Faith* (Jefferson, MD: The Trinity Foundation, 1983).

This is an excellent statement and should be defended against Berkhof's previous contrary assertions.[11]

Has Grudem read John Robbins, another Calvinist, who wrote a compelling article defending the idea that all faith is propositional?[12] Robbins wrote:

Truth is propositional, and only propositional. To put it even more plainly, truth is a property, characteristic, or attribute only of propositions. This view is in stark contrast to views, both academic and popular, of truth as encounter, truth as event, truth as pictorial, truth as experiential, truth as emotive, truth as personal, truth as mystic absorption into or union with the divine.

This last view, that truth is personal, not propositional, has led theologians to substitute the nebulous concepts of "commitment," "personal relationship," and "union" for the clear and Biblical concept of belief, thus undermining the Gospel itself.[13]

It sounds like Robbins has been reading Grudem, but Robbins wrote that in 2005. He concluded:

According to Scripture, truth is always and only propositional. There is nothing in Scripture that states or implies that truth is

---

[11] Ibid, 107, italics his.
[12] John Robbins, "The Biblical View of Truth," *The Trinity Review*, Feb-Mar 2005, 1-8.
[13] Ibid., 2.

encounter, event, picture, image, or emotion. Passages that seem to imply that something other than propositions is truth turn out to be figurative uses of the word truth. If the Gospel is to be preserved and propagated, it can be preserved only within the framework of literal, propositional truth, for salvation is, in the words of the Apostle Paul, "to come to the knowledge of the truth" (1 Timothy 2:4).[14]

One would think that in a book that is responding to FGT the author would at least be aware of and cite key books and articles cited by FGT. Many FG authors, myself included, have cited Clark and Robbins.

Grudem mentions GES and me again at the end of this section. When he does, he demonstrates that he lacks awareness of the significant discussions that have occurred in FGT. He writes:

I should add, however, that the Grace Evangelical Society and the Free Grace Alliance differ somewhat on this point [faith as trust]. The Grace Evangelical Society, under the leadership of Robert Wilkin, repeatedly emphasizes only believing the facts of the gospel (believing that I am a sinner and that Christ died to pay for my sins), with little or no mention of the need to go beyond belief that those facts are true and put one's trust in the person of Jesus Christ. By contrast, the materials promoted by the Free Grace Alliance do affirm in several places that our trust must

---

[14] Ibid., 8.

be placed in the person of Christ, not merely in facts about him (p. 105).

In the first place, neither GES nor the FGA believe or teach that a person who believes he is a sinner and that Christ died to pay for his sins is born again.[15] That is not the saving message. People who believe in works salvation also believe those things and yet are unregenerate.

In the second place, some in the FGA have criticized Zane Hodges and GES for suggesting that the object of saving faith is not the cross or empty tomb, but the Lord's promise that whoever believes in Him has everlasting life.[16]

Hodges taught, and GES teaches, that the cross and resurrection should lead people to believe the promise of life.[17] They are evidence the promise is true, but not equivalent to the promise itself.

---

[15] There are some FGA members who hold that, but they are in the minority. See, for example, J. B. Hixson, Rick Whitmire, and Roy Zuck, Editors, *Freely by His Grace* (Duluth, MN: Grace Gospel Press, 2012), 76, where George Meisinger, one of the contributors, writes, "Apparently Wilkin rejects the idea that believing Jesus died for one's sins is a sufficient object for saving faith."

[16] Thomas L. Stegall was a member of the FGA when he wrote *The Gospel of the Christ: A Biblical Response to the Crossless Gospel Regarding the Contents of Saving Faith* (Milwaukee, WI: Grace Gospel Press, 2009). Fred Lybrand, one of the founders of the FGA and its first Executive Director, wrote a 37-page open letter while he was the President of the FGA. In that letter he criticized Hodges and GES over this issue. See freegracefreespeech.googlepages.com/GESGospel. LybrandOpenLetter.04-14-09.pdf (accessed 12/23/2016). For responses from GES see Don Reiher, "Zane Hodges and GES Did Not Change the Gospel," *JOTGES* (Spring 2010): 31-58, and Robert N. Wilkin, "Another Look at the Deserted Island Illustration," *JOTGES* (Spring 2013): 3-20.

[17] See the articles by Reiher and Wilkin cited in the previous note.

You can believe that Jesus died and rose again and also believe in salvation by works.

In the third place, some in the FGA do not believe that assurance is of the essence of saving faith.[18] All in GES believe that in order to be born again one must believe the promise that the salvation/life/justification he receives by faith alone, apart from works, is secure forever and cannot be lost.[19]

Both Groups Deemphasize the Element of Heartfelt Trust in the Living Person of Christ

Adjectives are especially important in Grudem's understanding of saving faith. Trust must be *heartfelt*. The object of that *heartfelt trust* must not merely be Christ or the Person of Christ, but *the living Person of Christ*. This allows Grudem to make saving faith subjective and relative.

What is "heartfelt trust in the living Person of Christ"?

Grudem does not say, probably because he is convinced that "saving faith" is a mysterious existential encounter.

For example, Grudem speaks of saving faith as

---

[18] See David R. Anderson, "Is Belief in Eternal Security Necessary for Justification?" *Chafer Theological Seminary Journal* (Spring 2008): 47-59. Anderson was the President of the FGA when this article was published.
[19] Zane C. Hodges, "We Believe in Assurance," *JOTGES* (Autumn 1990): 3-17. One section is entitled, "IV. Assurance Is an Inseparable Part of Saving Faith" (pp. 11-16). The same article appeared again in a memorial issue: *JOTGES* (Spring 2009): 13-30. Both are available online at www. faithalone.org, s.v., Resources/Journal.

> …coming into the presence of the person of Christ and trusting him. The more you talk about the need for trust in the *person* of Christ the more you have to talk about a *personal encounter* with Christ, about coming into his very presence, and that means realizing deeply that he is your God (p. 106, italics his).

Grudem continues:

> The more we emphasize coming into the presence of Christ and trusting him, the more the idea of optional submission to his lordship becomes unthinkable. When we truly realize what it is to come into the majestic presence of the risen Christ, any thought of saying, 'Jesus, I'll trust you as my Savior today, and later I might decide to turn from sin and follow you,' is as far from our mind as the uttermost part of the sea (p. 106).

Robbins could have been speaking about Grudem when he wrote,

> [the] view that truth is personal, not propositional, has led theologians to substitute the nebulous concepts of "commitment," "personal relationship," and "union" for the clear and Biblical concept of belief, thus undermining the Gospel itself.[20]

Of course, assurance of one's eternal destiny is impossible if the issue is "a personal encounter,"

---

[20] Robbins, "The Biblical View of Truth," 2.

"submission to his lordship," and "turn[ing] from sin and follow[ing] [Christ]." Grudem touches on assurance at the end of this section:

> On the other hand, if saving faith involves more than just intellectual agreement that some statements in the Bible are true—if it also includes trusting Christ as a living person—*that is not quite so easy to determine.* It opens the question of whether an individual has really trusted Christ or not. *It makes the question of whether a person has genuine faith more complex* (pp. 106-107, italics added).

It is an understatement to say that Grudem's Lordship Salvation views make assurance of one's eternal destiny "more complex" and "not easy to determine." However, Grudem is trying to put the best spin on his view as possible.

In reality, his view makes assurance of one's eternal destiny *impossible*, since it requires two subjective elements, feelings and works.

Hodges could have been responding to Grudem when back in 1990 he ended an article on assurance saying, "So after all, if I have God's Word for something, what else do I need?"[21]

Grant Richison likewise says,

> Faith always rests on certainty, not on a suggestion of probability. Otherwise, chance is final and probability is empty. The very idea of probability precludes certainty and

---

[21] Hodges, "We Believe in Assurance," 17.

places chance at the core of a system…God's self-attesting Word transcends all probable approaches to truth.[22]

Mental Agreement with Facts *about* Christ, Without Personal Trust in Christ, Is Not Saving Faith

The fourth section in Chap. 4 is a restatement of the third section. I suppose what Grudem intends to do in this section is give proofs of what he already said in section three. His proofs fail to prove, however.

His first proof is that "saving faith is pictured as coming to Christ" (pp. 107-108). FGT heartily agrees. However, Grudem then says that "to 'come to' a person implies interpersonal interaction" (p. 107). Three times on one page he says that saving faith involves "personal interaction" (p. 108). He concludes his first proof by saying, "A personal encounter is in view" (p. 108).

Those are the words of postmodernity, not Biblical Christianity. Postmodernity reduces faith to personal encounters, feelings, and probabilities. The Bible indicates that faith is being convinced that what God has said is true.

R. C. Sproul is not a proponent of FGT. He even believes that a personal response of repentance and submission is necessary to be born again.[23] Yet he very

---

[22] Grant Richison, *Certainty: A Place to Stand* (Pickering, ON: Castle Quay Books, 2010), 259.

[23] R. C. Sproul, *Faith Alone: The Evangelical Doctrine of Justification* (Grand Rapids, MI: Baker Books, 1995), 168-71.

much rejects Grudem's idea that saving faith is a non-propositional personal encounter with Jesus:

> We live in an era that boasts of its vehement resistance to propositional truth. Truth is said to be a "relationship" or "personal encounter." Existential philosophy has placed so much stress on the personal and relational character of faith that an allergy has developed against propositional or objective truth.[24]

Believing in Jesus is propositional. He promises everlasting life to all who believe in Him. Do you believe that proposition (John 11:26)? That is, do you believe Him?

The second proof Grudem provides is that "saving faith is pictured as receiving Christ" (p. 108). He cites John 1:11-12. Grudem, without any Biblical support, says, "A personal encounter with Jesus Christ is in view" (p. 109). Yet those verses define *receiving* Jesus as "*believing* in His name."

His third line of proof is that "saving faith is pictured as believing something in your heart" (p. 109). He cites Rom 10:9-10. Grudem then announces, "Paul does not say 'believe in your mind'" (p. 109).

But Grudem misunderstands Paul.

In Rom 12:2 Paul spoke of being transformed, "by the renewing *of your mind*." In 2 Cor 3:14 and 4:4 he speaks of Satan blinding *the minds* of people. The words *heart* and *mind* are often used interchangeably in the New Testament to refer to the place where belief occurs. Sorg writes, "A striking feature of the New Testament is

---

[24] Ibid., 77.

the essential closeness of *kardia* [heart] to the concept *nous*, mind."[25]

Grudem's fourth line of proof is that "saving faith is portrayed as believing in a person" (p. 109). Grudem gives a highly misleading quotation from BDAG. The first meaning listed in this case is the one which is most prevalent in the New Testament. Yet Grudem gives *the second meaning* first and implies that BDAG says that all uses of *pisteuō* in John fall under that meaning. But actually BDAG lists about an even number of uses in John under definition one and two. And their placement of specific verses is not gospel. It is one man's evaluation. In fact, in the previous edition of BDAG, called BAGD (1979), there is no reference to commitment or total commitment in the second meaning (p. 661). It was added to the later edition.

Worse still, Grudem fails to point out what all Bible scholars know—that *pisteuō eis* (*believe in*) is used synonymously with *pisteuō hoti* (*believe that*) in the Fourth Gospel. This is clear in John 11:25-27 where the Lord refers to *pisteuō eis* twice and Martha responds with an affirmation using *pisteuō hoti*. It is also found in the famous theme verse of John 20:30-31. *To believe in* Jesus is *to believe that* He is the Christ, the Son of God. That is, it is to believe that He guarantees everlasting life to all who simply believe in Him for it (John 11:25-26 as compared with John 11:27).

My father used to promise he'd come to my football, basketball, and baseball games. At first *I believed in him*. That is, *I believed that he would indeed come* to my

---

[25] *New International Dictionary of New Testament Theology*, vol. 2, s.v., "Heart," 182. See also "Mind," 616-20.

games as he promised. But after one failure to fulfill his promise after another, I no longer believed in him. That is, I no longer believed that he would keep his promises. The alcohol had too strong of a hold on his life. He came occasionally. But often he did not.

Believing in a person is believing that he will fulfill his promises. It is not a personal encounter. It is not submission, partial or total, to the person.

Grudem reads his Lordship Salvation Theology into his understanding of Scripture.

Free Grace Misunderstandings of B. B. Warfield on the Need to Decide to Trust Christ Personally

This fifth and final proof is no proof at all. So what if some in FGT have misunderstood B. B. Warfield's view on saving faith? Warfield, as prominent a theologian as he was, did not write Scripture. His books are not inerrant. Whether Anderson and Dillow have rightly or wrongly understood Warfield is beside the point.

The point is, in Scripture, unbelief is a choice, while belief is not a choice. That is, while you can choose to ignore, avoid, or reject the proclamation of God's Word (Acts 13:46; see also John 5:39-40), strictly speaking, you cannot choose to believe it. You're either persuaded by the evidence, or not.

Of course, for Grudem, faith is not believing anyway, but a "personal encounter" as he repeats at the end of this chapter (p. 118). But how does one choose to have a *personal encounter* with the God of the universe?

Grudem never says.

Unlikely Interpretations?

Introduction

IN CHAPTER 5, Grudem considers eleven passages which he believes FGT has misinterpreted. After four chapters with very little, if any, exegesis, I was looking forward to how he actually interprets the Word of God.

In his final chapter, Grudem makes the odd claim that FGT diminishes the gospel because it holds what he calls *unlikely interpretations.*

Unlikely according to whom? Reformed theologians?

Did Luther and Calvin diminish the gospel because their interpretations were considered very unlikely by nearly all the Catholic and Orthodox theologians and priests of their day?

I'll grant that Grudem's interpretations of these eleven passages are consistent with those of the majority of Calvinist scholars today. But that is not relevant because truth is not determined by consensus.[1] What

---

[1] If truth was determined by consensus, then Christianity would not be true. For every person on earth today who identifies himself as a Christian (31.5%, which is surely more than actually are born again) there

matters is which interpretation makes best sense of Scripture. So I will evaluate his interpretations based on the words of Scripture.

Grudem's selection of passages includes one from the Synoptic Gospels, one from John (which he split into two separate discussions), three from Acts, two from Paul's epistles, and three from James.[2]

Surprisingly, Grudem cites only one FGT author in ten of the eleven passages, namely, Zane Hodges. Chapter 5 should be entitled, "Some Examples of Unlikely Interpretations by Zane Hodges."

Since Grudem's book is about FGT, why doesn't he discuss the views of Jody Dillow, Dave Anderson, Charlie Bing, Charles Ryrie, Tom Constable, John Hart, R. B. Thieme, Fred Chay, Earl Radmacher, Gary Derickson, Elliott Johnson, or me?[3]

While I agree with most of the interpretations of Zane Hodges, a book on FGT should not focus only on his views, any more than a book on Calvinism should focus solely on Grudem's views.

---

are a little over two people who identify themselves as non-Christians, including Muslim (23.2%), Irreligious (16.3 %), Hindu (15%), Buddhist (7.1%), Folk Religion (5.9%), and Other Religion (1%).

[2] Aren't these choices odd? Why no passages from John 1-12, often called "The Book of Signs"? Why only two from Paul? Why three from James? Why none from Peter, Hebrews, and 1-3 John? Why nothing from the justification section in Romans 3-4? Why nothing from Galatians, Paul's defense of his gospel?

[3] Of course, he might also discuss the views of early FGT writers, such as John Glas, Robert Sandeman, the Marrow Men, and J. N. Darby.

They Will Repent (Luke 16:30)

> "And he said, 'No, father Abraham; but if one
> goes to them from the dead, they will repent.'"

Grudem's interpretation. Grudem says that this verse
"implies that the brothers need to repent in order to be
saved" (p. 120).

Grudem's explanation of the FGT interpretation.
Grudem mentions that Zane Hodges argues the rich
man was incorrect. Thus the FGT view (assuming
there is but one FGT interpretation of this verse, which
is false) is that the rich man mistakenly believed the
condition of everlasting life is repentance.

Grudem responds to the view of Hodges:

> But that understanding of the verse is certainly
> wrong, for in the next verse Jesus himself
> assumes that the brothers need repentance,
> when he has Abraham say[4] that they would not
> even be convinced "if someone should rise from
> the dead" (Luke 16:31). Jesus's [*sic*] argument
> about their culpability would not be persuasive
> unless the reader assumes that they needed to
> be "convinced" of the thing that has just been
> mentioned, the need to repent (pp. 120-21).

Grudem's reasoning is hard to grasp. Abraham
was not talking about the rich man's statement that his

---

[4] Jesus does not "have Abraham say" anything. Grudem calls Luke 16:19-
31 "Jesus's [*sic*] parable" (p. 120). Thus he thinks Jesus made up this
whole story. He thinks it never happened. Yet neither the Lord nor Luke
call it a parable. And no other parable gives a proper name. This account
has two proper names, Lazarus and Abraham.

brothers would repent if someone came back from the dead. Before the rich man's comment, Abraham had said, "They have Moses and the prophets; let them hear them" (Luke 16:29). Notice the words, "let them hear them." Hearing Moses and the prophets would mean believing what they wrote about the Messiah, that is, about Jesus. The expression *Moses and the Prophets* occurs twice more in Luke (24:27, 44), once in John (1:45), and once in Acts (28:23). In all of these cases *Moses and the Prophets* prove that Jesus is the Messiah. None of those contexts even mention repentance.

After the rich man's comment, Abraham said again, "If they do not hear Moses and the prophets, neither will they be persuaded though one rise from the dead."

Abraham was talking about the need to *believe* the witness of Moses and the prophets concerning *Messiah*, that is, *Jesus*. Three times Abraham spoke of believing in Jesus: "let them hear them" (v 29), "If they will not hear Moses and the prophets" (v 31a), and "neither will they be persuaded though one rise from the dead" (v 31b). *Hearing* and *being persuaded* are synonyms for *believing*.

Abraham spoke of *believing*. The rich man spoke of *repenting*. And then Abraham again spoke about believing.

Abraham said nothing about repenting. He pointed to God's Word and the witness to Jesus that is found there. Let them hear that witness, that is, let them believe in Jesus in light of the witness of Moses and the prophets. Yet Grudem thinks that Abraham was discussing repentance, not faith.

Are we to understand that the unregenerate man got it right, and the regenerate man—the great patriarch of the faith, Abraham—got it wrong?

Darrell Bock, who does not hold to FGT, contradicts Grudem's interpretation: "It is necessary to respond to Jesus with belief, since there is no other name under heaven by which it is *necessary* to be saved (Acts 4:12; cf. Luke 16:30-31)."[5]

Grudem's understanding of Luke 19:16-31 is not consistent with the text. Abraham did not *validate* what the rich man said; he *corrected* him.

It is Grudem's view, not the view of FGT, which is an unlikely interpretation.

Branches Taken Away (John 15:1-2)

> "I am the true vine, and My Father is the vinedresser. Every branch in Me that does not bear fruit He takes away [or He lifts up], and every branch that bears fruit He prunes, that it may bear more fruit."

Grudem's interpretation. He says, "This passage creates a difficulty for the Free Grace position because it shows that if someone's life is unfruitful, that person will be taken away from Christ, who is the true vine" (p. 121).

What does Grudem mean? What does *being taken away from Christ* mean?

Grudem seems to be saying that the correct interpretation of John 15:1-2 is that if a believer's life is unfruitful, then he will lose everlasting life. What else

---

[5] Darrell L. Bock, *A Theology of Luke and Acts* (Grand Rapids, MI: Zondervan, 2012), 140, emphasis his. See also Leon Morris, *Luke* (Grand Rapids, MI: Eerdmans, 1974, 1988), 278.

could Grudem's phrase *taken away from Christ* mean,
since only a believer is *in Christ*? An unbeliever is not
in Christ, so he cannot be *taken away from Christ*.

Grudem's explanation of the FGT interpretation.
Grudem wrongly suggests that it is the uniform view
of FGT that what is in view here is the lifting up of
the unfruitful branch, not its being taken away. *Some*
do hold to the lifting-up view (e.g., Radmacher and
Derickson).[6] However, others think this could be
teaching what John 15:6 says, that is, that it refers to
temporal judgment—God's discipline and judgment in
this life. It is not essential to FGT to take *airō* as *lift up*
in John 15:2. Hodges, for example, did not take it that
way.[7]

It is quite surprising that Grudem does not mention
Hodges's interpretation of this passage. He cites Hodges
as his only source in the other ten passages, so why not
here?

Grudem argues that in first century viticulture,
unfruitful branches were never *lifted up*. He suggests
that they were *taken away* to be burned and that burning
refers to eternal condemnation.

His discussion of this subject is imprecise.

For example, see note 5 on p. 122. Grudem says
that pruning weak, broken, or diseased branches "is the
opposite of saying that branches that do not bear fruit

---

[6] See Earl D. Radmacher and Gary W. Derickson, *The Disciplemaker*
(Salem, OR: Charis Press, 2001).

[7] See Zane C. Hodges, "1 John," *The Bible Knowledge Commentary*, ed.
John F. Walvoord and Roy B. Zuck (Wheaton, IL: Victor, 1983), 2:888-
89). See also Zane C. Hodges, *Absolutely Free: A Biblical Reply to Lordship Salvation*, Second Edition (Corinth, TX: Grace Evangelical Society,
2014), 118-21.

are 'lifted up' so that they may bear more fruit." The opposite? The two ideas are unrelated. Branches which are not bearing fruit can be healthy, unbroken, and not diseased. Pruning is not the same as lifting up.

Strangely, Grudem does not discuss the very next verse, John 15:3, in which the Lord says, "You are already clean because of the word which I have spoken to you." Doesn't that verse mean the disciples, to whom He is addressing this discussion of fruitfulness, were eternally secure? If not, why not?

The Lord had already promised the eleven that they would sit on thrones and rule over the twelve tribes of Israel (Matt 19:28, with Matthias taking Judas' place as Acts 1:15-26 says). Thus this cannot be a warning that *they* would be eternally condemned.

Can *anyone* who is a branch and is connected to the vine, which is Jesus, be eternally condemned? No. But Grudem says that can happen. How does this fit his Calvinism?

Why would the Lord only give one option for dealing with unfruitful branches? If it is possible to stimulate unfruitful branches so that they might become fruitful, would that not be desirable and wise?

Grudem seems to be saying that it is impossible for unfruitful believers to become fruitful. If so, why? Is it not possible for God to turn an unfruitful branch into a fruitful one?

It is hard to see why Grudem discusses John 15:1-2, given the fact that he also discusses John 15:6, which he interprets as saying the same thing.

Grudem's interpretation of John 15:1-2 is more than unlikely—it's impossible, because loss of everlasting

life is impossible. Compare John 5:24; 6:35; 11:26;
15:3.

Branches Thrown in the Fire (John 15:6)

"If anyone does not abide in Me, he is cast out
as a branch and is withered; and they gather
them and throw them into the fire, and they are
burned."

Grudem's interpretation. Grudem admits he
interprets this verse the same as he did John 15:1-2:
"This passage continues Jesus's [*sic*] *same teaching*
about vine and branches..." (p. 123, emphasis added).

Grudem's explanation of the FGT interpretation.
He has two paragraphs about Hodges's interpretation of
John 15:6. He says that Hodges understands the burning
to refer to temporal judgment, not eternal condemnation.

It is true that Hodges says that the burning in
John 15:6, "portray[s] divine chastening as a fire."[8]
But Grudem fails to mention that Hodges also said
that believers who ceased to abide in Christ "would
be separated from their experience of fellowship with
Him."[9] Readers should take the time to read what
Hodges actually said about this passage.[10] Grudem
rejects as out of hand the idea that temporal judgment is
in view here.

Grudem says that being thrown into the fire and
burned is a "picture of final judgment" (p. 123). Hence,

---

[8] Hodges, *Absolutely Free*, 121.
[9] Ibid., 120.
[10] Ibid., 118-23.

Grudem understands the Lord to be warning Peter, James, John, Matthew, and the other disciples—and all disciples of Christ—that they might be sent to the lake of fire.

Grudem suggests that the burning of vegetation in Scripture is *always* total and *must* refer to eternal condemnation. He mentions one New Testament and ten Old Testament passages to support his conclusion. However, he does not quote them, or discuss them, and if you look them up you will find they do not support his claim at all.

For example, in Matt 3:12, the Lord refers to "unquenchable fire" and uses a stronger Greek word that means "burn up." Whereas John 15:6 has *kaiō* ("they are burned"), Matt 3:12 has *katakaiō* ("He will burn up"). While Hodges discusses the difference between these two Greek words, Grudem does not.

Grudem inexplicably cites Isa 9:18, which says, "wickedness burns as the fire; it shall devour the briers and thorns…" That is a reference to the destructive nature of wickedness. It is not a reference to the lake of fire.

Another puzzling proof text he cites is Lev 6:12, which says, "the fire on the altar shall be kept burning on it." That fire stopped in AD 70. In any case, that verse has nothing to do with John 15:6.

I urge interested readers to look up all the passages Grudem mentions. He gives examples of the burning of wooden idols, embers on an altar, chariots, the wood of the vine, and branches. But these all illustrate temporal judgment, not eternal condemnation. In other words, he actually is arguing *against his own position*, and supporting the Free Grace interpretation. The more verses you look up, the weaker his case becomes (e.g., Lev 13:52, 57; Deut 7:5; 12:3; Josh 11:6; Jer 4:2, 22 [neither of which even mentions fire]; Ezek 15:4-6; 19:12).

Grudem's interpretation that born-again people (i.e., clean people, John 15:3), will be eternally condemned if they fail to produce enough good works is not just unlikely, but impossible. No believer will be judged regarding his eternal destiny as the Lord clearly promised in John 5:24 ("he shall not come into judgment"). Believers are eternally secure.[11]

Repentance to Life (Acts 11:18)

> When they heard these things they became silent; and they glorified God, saying, "Then God has granted to the Gentiles repentance to life."

Grudem's interpretation. He says, "People become Christians through 'repentance that leads to life'" (p. 125).

Grudem's explanation of the FGT interpretation. He claims that Hodges teaches that "repentance leads to some additional level of fellowship or discipleship after salvation" (p. 125). He does not quote Hodges to support that claim. Actually, Hodges did not believe or teach that there are levels of fellowship. Fellowship is absolute. One is either in fellowship with God or not. As cited above,

---

[11] See Leon Morris, *The Gospel According to John* (Grand Rapids, MI: Eerdmans, 1971), 671. He says, "These are strong words which empha-size the necessity of remaining in vital contact with Christ if fruitfulness is to continue."

Hodges wrote, "If they failed to 'abide' in Jesus, they would be separated from the experience of fellowship with Him."[12]

Nor did Hodges ever say that there are *additional levels of discipleship.*

Hodges cited the prodigal son and Rom 8:13 and said that "'coming to life' is always the end result of repentance, whether it be the repentance of a Christian or the repentance of the unsaved."[13] Hodges spoke of the unsaved repenting and coming to life. Grudem said that Hodges was only talking about a Christian's super level of fellowship or discipleship. That is incorrect.

Personally, I am not sure what Peter's companions meant. Hodges may be correct; however, I think another view is more likely. Peter's companions might well have been saying that repentance leads to *everlasting life.* Grudem fails to mention my view, which is in print.[14]

Peter's friends were likely saying that repentance can be a way in which someone comes to faith in Christ for everlasting life. By turning from one's sins, he becomes more open to going to church, prayer, listening to a Christian, etc. Repentance can be a step toward God that ultimately results in faith in Christ for everlasting life.

Luke was not citing Peter's companions in order to contradict what Peter said to Cornelius, i.e., believe in Jesus (Acts 10:43; 11:14; 15:7-11).[15] Peter did not call

---

[12] Hodges, *Absolutely Free*, 120.

[13] Ibid., 136.

[14] Robert N. Wilkin, *The Ten Most Misunderstood Words in the Bible* (Denton, TX: Grace Evangelical Society, 2012), 117-18.

[15] It is possible that Peter's companions were wrong and they meant that repentance is the condition, or a condition, of everlasting life. In that case, I would think Peter would have corrected them on the spot. Compare Acts 15:7-11 in which Peter retells this incident with Cornelius.

upon Cornelius to repent. Grudem seems to think he did.

Indeed, F. F. Bruce suggests yet another view. He thinks that *repentance unto life* refers to God "giving them [Gentiles] the change of heart and mind which results in eternal life."[16]

Grudem's main support amounts to circular reasoning: "the entire structure of the book of Acts" teaches that repentance is a condition of everlasting life (p. 125). Grudem cites Acts 1:8 (p. 125) and Acts 11:14 (p. 126) to support his claim. However, it is hard to see how either Acts 1:8 or 11:14 supports that.

What about Acts 16:30-31? When Paul was asked, "What must I do to be saved?" his answer was "Believe on the Lord Jesus Christ and you shall be saved..." He did not mention repentance. Why not?

What about Acts 10:1-47? Peter speaks of faith in Christ as the condition (Acts 10:43), without mentioning repentance.

What about Acts 15:7-11? At the Jerusalem Council, Peter summarizes his experience with Cornelius; he speaks of faith in Christ and does not mention repentance.

What about Acts 13:46, 48? The issue in Paul's first recorded sermon in Acts is faith in Christ, not repentance, which he doesn't even mention.

Although Grudem thinks the FGT interpretations are unlikely, his interpretation is out of step with the Word of God.

---

[16] F. F. Bruce, *Commentary on the Book of Acts* (Grand Rapids, MI: Eerdmans, 1981), 236.

God Commanded All to Repent (Acts 17:30)

"Truly, these times of ignorance God
overlooked, but now commands all men
everywhere to repent..."

Grudem's interpretation. He understands Paul to say
that repentance is "necessary to escape final judgment"
(p. 127).

Grudem's explanation of the FGT interpretation.
Grudem cites Hodges as saying that repentance is
necessary "to enter into harmonious relationship with
God" (p. 126).

According to Grudem,

Acts 17 is a summary of Paul's initial gospel
proclamation to the philosophers in Athens.
And in this initial gospel message, the one and
only thing he says that God commands is that
they repent (p. 126).

The first half of Acts 17 concerns Paul's ministry
in Thessalonica and Berea, not in Athens as Grudem
mistakenly says. Even Acts 17:16-21 says nothing about
Paul's gospel proclamation in Athens.

Grudem evidently means that Acts 17:22-34 (and
more particularly, Acts 17:30-34), is a summary of Paul's
"initial gospel message" (p. 126).

What do the words "initial gospel message" and
"initial gospel proclamation" mean? Are there different
saving messages? Did Paul preach an *initial saving
message* only to later come back with a different one?

Hopefully what Grudem means is that Paul was
doing *pre-evangelism* here. He was pointing people to

Jesus and telling them that Jesus will judge the world on some future day. Repentance is all that is mentioned. Paul doesn't mention faith in Christ, the new birth, everlasting life, justification, the cross of Christ, or anything else associated with his normal preaching.

If so, I agree this is pre-evangelism. We are told by Luke in Acts 17:34 that "some men joined him and believed." Luke did not say, "some men believed and joined him." The message in Acts 17:30 generated interest. Some people said, "We will hear you again on this matter" (Acts 17:33). They heard more from Paul when they joined him, and as a result, they believed. It was then that Paul preached the message of life, and they believed.

Darrell Bock agrees, saying,

> Paul never gets to the full presentation of the gospel because the resurrection leads to discussion, but Luke in this speech gives a kind of prolegomena for how to present God to someone who lacks background about the one true God.[17]

It is odd that Grudem does not comment on Acts 17:33-34. Why does Luke say that "some men... *believed*"? Shouldn't he have said, "Some men... *repented*"? If repentance is the condition of eternal life, then why mention faith and fail to mention repentance? Notice that Paul did not say, "God has commanded all men everywhere to repent *so that they will have everlasting life.*" Nor did he say, "the one who repents has everlasting life." Grudem said that, but not Paul. Did the

---

[17] Bock, *Luke and Acts*, 117.

men in Acts 17:34 also repent? Possibly. But Luke does not tell us.

So why does Paul say that God has commanded all men to repent? Because God commanded it. Paul's ministry was not merely one of evangelism. It also included calling unbelievers and believers to turn from their sins and to follow Christ in discipleship.

Works Befitting Repentance (Acts 26:19-20)

"Therefore, King Agrippa, I was not disobedient to the heavenly vision, but declared first to those in Damascus and in Jerusalem, and throughout all the region of Judea, and then to the Gentiles, that they should repent, turn to God, and do works befitting repentance."

Grudem's interpretation. "That is Paul's summary… of his entire preaching ministry both to Jews and to Gentiles" (p. 127). He then concludes from that statement that "repentance [is] a necessary part of the initial gospel message" (p. 127).

Grudem's explanation of the FGT interpretation. He cites Hodges as suggesting that Paul "is explaining how to live a life of holiness and good works *after* one is saved" (p. 127). Yet the quote from Hodges which Grudem provides does not say anything about *after one is saved*. Hodges was merely saying that Paul was seeking to turn people to God and to do good works.

Grudem's position is unlikely in the extreme. Are we to understand that an accurate summary of Paul's entire preaching ministry would leave out calling people to faith in Christ? How does Grudem explain Acts

20:21, "testifying to Jews, and also to Greeks, repentance toward God and faith toward our Lord Jesus Christ"? Is that not a summary of Paul's entire preaching ministry?

No one disputes that Paul, the other Apostles, and the Lord Himself all called people to repent. But that does not establish that repentance is the condition for everlasting life. We are called to do many things that are not conditions of eternal salvation.

Acts 26:19-20 does not mention salvation, everlasting life, or faith in Christ. If this is Paul's summary of his entire preaching ministry, wouldn't it be odd for him to leave out the call to faith and the promise of everlasting life?

Confess and Believe (Romans 10:9-13)

That if you confess with your mouth the Lord Jesus and believe in your heart that God has raised Him from the dead, you will be saved. For with the heart one believes unto righteousness, and with the mouth confession is made unto salvation. For the Scripture says, *"Whoever believes on Him will not be put to shame."* For there is no distinction between Jew and Greek, for the same Lord over all is rich to all who call upon Him. For *"whoever calls on the name of the Lord shall be saved"* (emphasis added).

Grudem's interpretation. He says that the salvation in vv 9, 10, and 13 is eternal salvation from hell, not deliverance from God's wrath in this life.

Grudem's explanation of the FGT interpretation. He cites Hodges as saying that "calling on the name of the Lord to be saved (v 13) does not mean calling out to gain eternal salvation, but calling out 'to obtain His aid and deliverance in daily life'" (p. 129).

Grudem fails to explain *why* Hodges takes that interpretation or *how* Hodges defends his view.

If v 13 refers to an *unbeliever* calling out to the Lord for everlasting life, then what does v 14 mean? There Paul writes, "How then shall they call on Him *in whom they have not believed?*"

Paul is not talking about *unbelievers* who call upon the Lord. He is discussing *believers* who call upon Him.

Notice that each of the three questions in v 14 states an effect and then the prior cause. The effect of "calling on Him" is based on the prior cause of believing in Him: "How then shall they call on Him in whom they have not [already] believed?"

In other words, belief precedes calling. But Grudem does not quote or discuss Rom 10:14.

Hence the ones doing the calling in v 13 are *believers*, not *unbelievers*. And if they are believers, they are already eternally saved. Thus the salvation of v 13 is not salvation from eternal condemnation (since believers are already delivered from that).

Grudem does not mention or discuss the fact that the quote in v 13 is from Joel 2:32. Is he suggesting that Joel 2:32 is an Old Testament evangelistic verse? Actually, Joel 2:32 deals with the Tribulation and states that believing Jews who call on the name of the Lord will be saved from dying.

Grudem also fails to explain how confessing Christ (calling on His name) can be a requirement

for everlasting life. That is not a requirement he has
mentioned before.

So now the conditions for having everlasting life
are repentance, heartfelt trust, personal encounter, *and
public confession of Christ?*

Is that list complete?

Are there more requirements Grudem has not yet
mentioned?

Examine Yourselves (2 Corinthians 13:5)

Examine yourselves as to whether you are in
the faith. Test yourselves. Do you not know
yourselves, that Jesus Christ is in you?—unless
indeed you are disqualified.

Grudem's interpretation. Grudem understands this
verse to be a call for the readers to "examine themselves
to find out if they are really born again or not" (p. 131).
For evidence he cites the words "in the faith" and "that
Jesus Christ is in you" (pp. 131-32).

Grudem's explanation of the FGT interpretation.
He cites Hodges as saying that the issue is not whether
they are born again, but "whether they are 'living in a
dynamic, faith-oriented connection with Jesus Christ'"
(p. 131).

Grudem does not discuss the fact that 2 Cor 13:5
is part of a context that runs from vv 1-6. In v 3 Paul
says, "you seek a proof of Christ speaking in me." When
he comes to v 5, Paul turns the tables on the readers
who were questioning whether he speaks for Christ.
The word *yourselves* is first in the Greek sentence for
emphasis: *Yourselves examine!* But note, they were

questioning his apostleship, not his eternal destiny. Likewise, in turning the tables, Paul is not asking them to question their eternal destiny, either. He has a different question in mind. But what?

Grudem fails to mention or discuss the Greek words *dokimos, adokimos,* and *dokimazō* which appear in vv 5-7.

"Test yourselves" is from *dokimazō*. At the end of that same verse Paul says, "unless you are disqualified." *Disqualified* translates the related adjective, *adokimos,* failing the test. Disqualified from what test? The test is whether or not a believer has lived a life worthy of the Lord's approval and reward.

Verse 6 picks up on the theme of vv 1-4, "But I trust you will know that we are not disqualified." Again, the word *disqualified* is the related adjective *adokimos*.

Then in v 7 the adjective *dokimos* occurs ("not that we should appear approved") and its antonym, *adokimos* ("though we may seem disqualified").

None of this is mentioned or discussed by Grudem. His interpretation ignores the context and is inconsistent with it.

Can Faith Save Him? (James 2:14-17)

What does it profit, my brethren, if someone says he has faith but does not have works? Can faith save him? If a brother or sister is naked and destitute of daily food, and one of you says to them, "Depart in peace, be warmed and filled," but you do not give them the things which are needed for the body, what does it

profit? Thus also faith by itself, if it does not
have works, is dead.

Grudem's interpretation. He understands James to
be saying that "genuine faith will always result in good
works," and that unless we add faith to our works we
cannot be saved from eternal condemnation (pp. 133-
34).

Grudem's explanation of the FGT interpretation.
He cites Hodges as saying that those addressed here are
born again therefore the salvation in view is salvation
from temporal judgment, not salvation from eternal
judgment (p. 133).

The evidence Grudem cites to support his position
are 1) James is not addressing most of his readers, just
"'someone' who may be in a different situation than
most of the readers" (p. 133), and 2) the salvation here
must be salvation from eternal condemnation since
"*sōzō*...always refers to eternal salvation except where
the context specifies a situation of rescue from physical
danger or healing from physical sickness (as in James
5:15 or Matt. 8:25; 9:22, for example)" (pp. 133-34).

The problems with Grudem's view are legion.

First of all, it is forced to suggest that James doesn't
have all his readers in mind when he says, "So speak
and so do as those who will be judged by the law
of liberty" (Jas 2:12). The same speaking and doing
command is found in 2:14 ("If someone says...but does
not have works [i.e., does not do]") and 2:16 ("One of
you says...but you do not give them the things which
are needed").

Second, he fails to recognize or comment on the
repeated phrase *ti to ophelos*, which starts v 14 and ends

v 16. "What does it profit?" or "What use is it?" is the question James has in mind, but Grudem does not.

Third, Grudem only discusses two of the uses of *sōzō* in James (2:14; 5:15) here.[18] Grudem concedes that 5:15 refers to physical salvation. What about 1:21; 4:12; and 5:20? Grudem does not mention or discuss James's three other uses of *sōzō*. They all refer to saving one's physical life from death. And all three are addressed to believers.

Fourth, Grudem is wrong to say that *sōzō* in James (and elsewhere) always refers to eternal salvation from hell *except* when the context explicitly indicates that healing or temporal deliverance is in view.[19] That is not a safe assumption. Moreover, the context *does* indicate that all five uses of *sōzō* in James refer to temporal deliverance. Grudem cannot see that because his theology will not allow it.

Fifth, and finally, Grudem discusses Jas 2:14-17 earlier in *5 Ways*. He writes,

> If a person has no good works, if there is no change in his life, then he has "dead faith"—and verse 14 implies that that kind of faith cannot save a person, because James expects the answer no when he asks the question, "Can that faith save him?" (p. 80).

---

[18] He does discuss Jas 5:19-20 later in the chapter. However, he does not mention that or summarize his findings here. See below for a discussion of his interpretation of Jas 5:19-20.

[19] For an excellent refutation of Grudem's claim, see Joseph Dillow, "Can Faith Save Him?" *A Defense of Free Grace Theology*, ed. Fred Chay (N.P.: Grace Theology Press, 2017), 151-55.

Grudem says that one is saved when he has living faith. And he says that one can't have living faith without good works. Grudem understands James to be saying that faith and good works are co-conditions for salvation from eternal condemnation. In other words, Grudem believes James is teaching salvation by faith plus works.

Grudem's interptation of Jas 2:14-17 is beyond unlikely.

Faith Without Works Is Dead (James 2:26)

> For as the body without the spirit is dead, so faith without works is dead also.

Grudem's interpretation. He suggests that faith without works is "dead faith" and not really faith at all. Hence the person who has faith without works is not born again because he lacks true faith, faith plus works (pp. 134-36). Again, this means a person doesn't become a "true believer" until he has good works. Since all "true believers" persevere in good works till death, salvation logically occurs after perseverance, not after a few months of good works.

Grudem's explanation of the FGT interpretation. He cites Hodges as saying that faith without works is faith which "has lost all of its vitality and productiveness" (p. 134).

To support his view, Grudem leans heavily on two things: 1) the entire passage is about salvation from eternal condemnation (see esp. Jas 2:14), and 2) dead faith is non-faith, faith that never has existed.

As discussed above, Grudem is wrong that the salvation in 2:14 refers to salvation from eternal condemnation.

In addition, he is wrong that "faith without works is dead" means "faith without works is not faith." That is illogical. Faith is faith. Faith without works is still faith. When James says that faith is *dead*, he clearly means it is *unprofitable* as shown by the twice repeated question, "What does it profit" (2:14, 16). To say that faith without works is not really faith is to contradict what James says and to miss his point.

The Lordship Salvation understanding of Jas 2:26, that is, Grudem's understanding, is illogical and contrary to the context.

Saving a Soul from Death (James 5:19-20)

> Brethren, if anyone among you wanders from the truth, and someone turns him back, let him know that he who turns a sinner from the error of his way will save a soul from death and cover a multitude of sins.

Grudem's interpretation. He suggests that James is saying that a Christian can save a straying false professor *from hell* by bringing him back from the spiritual far country (p. 137).

Grudem's explanation of the FGT interpretation. He cites Hodges as saying that a Christian can save a straying believer *from premature physical death* by bringing him back from the spiritual far country (p. 137).

Grudem only devotes two short paragraphs to both discuss the FGT view and explain his own. This is far less than he did on the other ten passages.

Grudem is convinced that salvation from eternal condemnation is in view in the closing verses of James, but he does not discuss what James means when he says, "he who turns a sinner from the error of his way will save a soul from death and cover a multitude of sins." Isn't he a bit concerned about saying that we can save our fellow brothers and sisters from hell? If they are believers, then they are already saved once and for all. They can't lose everlasting life, and we can't do anything to keep them saved. They are already secure. That is what ever-lasting life means (cf. John 5:24; 11:26).

John Piper is, like Grudem, a Calvinist who does not agree with FGT. However, his understanding of Jas 5:19-20 is inconsistent with that of Grudem.

Grudem believes that James is talking about Christians saving *false professors* from eternal condemnation by leading them to repentance:

> ...there are people "among you" (that is, in the church) who are professing Christians but are in danger of eternal condemnation, as shown by their sinful pattern of life. James urges his readers to care for such a person and try to bring him back from his "wandering," for this "will save his soul from death" (p. 137).

Grudem does not believe that true professors "are in danger of eternal condemnation." Only false believers are in such danger. For Grudem the wandering professing Christian is an unbeliever who needs to be saved eternally. Notice the future tense in his last sentence, when he quotes part of the text: "...this [bringing him back] 'will save his soul from death.'"

Piper gives much more detail and is much clearer. Piper believes that James is talking about Christians saving *fellow Christians, true professors*, from eternal condemnation by leading them to repentance. While I disagree with Piper that salvation from eternal condemnation is in view, I agree with him, contra Grudem, that James is clearly speaking of Christians rescuing actual Christians.

In the first of two sermons on Jas 5:19-20 at the desiringgod.org website, Piper says, "this [wandering] person is clearly a Christian, clearly he [James] is referring to brothers."

Shortly after that in the message Piper backtracks a bit, saying, "...a sinner in the mouth of James is a Christian—at least he is a professing Christian—and he is treating him as a Christian."

In part two of this message Piper says that God uses Christians to save fellow Christians from eternal condemnation. His fifth point in that message is "God keeps His children [eternally secure] by means of His children." He said, "We participate in each other's perseverance, and thus salvation. Eternal security is a community project."

In Piper's view, the person who will be saved from eternal condemnation is a person who is already saved, not an unbeliever. If that is confusing to you, it is because Piper believes in something called *final salvation*. A person is initially saved by faith alone in Christ alone. But, in order to gain *final salvation*, one must persevere in faith and good works. If one strays, it is essential that a fellow Christian bring him back in order for him to gain *final salvation*.

Piper's view of eternal security strikes me as denying eternal security. If one must persevere to gain *final salvation*, then he is clearly not finally saved right now.

Believers cannot save fellow believers from hell, but we can save one another from the temporal judgment that will fall if our beloved friends who have strayed do not repent.[20]

Grudem's interpretation is not only unlikely, it is impossible.

Conclusion

In Chapter 5, Wayne Grudem fails to show that FGT diminishes the gospel. Indeed, his exegesis of these eleven passages is so questionable that *his* interpretations should be called *unlikely*. Chapter 5 undermines his efforts to promote Lordship Salvation.

---

[20] Charles Ryrie says, "The death is physical death which sin may cause (1 Cor 11:30)," *Ryrie Study Bible* (Chicago, IL: Moody, 1976, 1978), 1863.

CHAPTER 6

Five Ways Grudem Diminishes the Gospel

Introduction

IF GRUDEM IS CORRECT, then FGT indeed diminishes the gospel and actually proclaims a false gospel. If one must do all the things that Grudem says to be born again, and Free Grace people say you don't need to do all those things, then we are proclaiming heresy.

But what if Grudem is wrong? Diminishing the gospel cuts both ways. If the only condition for regeneration is believing in Jesus for everlasting life, then Grudem is not only diminishing the gospel, he is abandoning it. In that case, he'd be against the grace of God.

There are five major ways in which Grudem diminishes the gospel.

He Makes Our Works, Not Jesus' Works, the Issue

First, Grudem underemphasizes Jesus' role in our salvation.

He does say that "Christ's work has earned salvation for sinners" and "Christ died and paid the penalty for our sins" (p. 85). But then he makes that work of lesser importance, saying,

> But that is not the question here. The question is not: How can I know that Christ has died for people's sins and that he will save all who believe in Him. The question is rather: How do I know *that I have truly believed* (p. 85, italics his).

Grudem's major concern in *5 Ways* is what *we can and must do for Jesus* in order to be saved and in order to have some measure of hope that we might be saved.

Grudem repeatedly says in *5 Ways* that in order to be born again we must turn from his sins, submit to Christ's Lordship, commit to obey Christ for the rest of our life, and find assurance that we have done those things by looking at all the good works we have done:

- We must decide to turn from our sin (pp. 38, 41-76, 146). "Repentance is a heartfelt sorrow for sin, a renouncing of it, and a sincere commitment to forsake it and walk in obedience to Christ" (p. 42).
- We must trust in Christ as a living person (pp. 99-118, 146). "The more we emphasize coming into the presence of Christ and trusting him, the more the idea of optional submission to his lordship [*sic*] becomes unthinkable" (p. 106).
- We need to sincerely receive Christ (pp. 52, 108, 146), which means we must have "a close

personal encounter with him who is the living Lord and God of the universe" (p. 52) and we must have a "deep, heartfelt repentance for [our] sins" (p. 53). "In the first century, to 'receive someone' would have meant welcoming that person into fellowship, into a relationship..." (p. 108).

- We need to see evident change in our lives (pp. 29, 38, 79-82, 84, 86-87, 89, 91, 146). "The faith that justifies is never alone because it never occurs by itself, but is always accompanied by— or includes—repentance from sin and is always followed by other actions such as doing good works and continuing to believe" (p. 38).

- We must submit and commit to the Lordship of Christ (pp. 42, 106). As cited above under the first bullet point, Grudem says to be born again one must have "a sincere commitment to...walk in obedience to Christ" (p. 42).

- Salvation is something which we must work to obtain and retain. Whereas Jesus and the Apostles spoke of salvation as a free gift which Jesus offers to the believer, Grudem does not. See Grudem's favorable quote of Schreiner below. In fact, the word *gift* and the words *free gift* are only used in this book when Grudem quotes Free Grace advocates such as Dave Anderson (pp. 84, 106 [note 13]), Zane Hodges (p. 82), and the Free Grace Alliance (p. 19 [note 1], 101).

Though a Calvinist, Grudem's *emphasis*, to use his own word, is on the submission (and subsequent obedience) we need to offer in order to gain everlasting life: "The more we emphasize coming into the presence of Christ and trusting him, the more the idea of optional submission to his lordship [*sic*] becomes unthinkable" (p. 106).

Grudem diminishes the gospel by placing his emphasis on what we do for Christ and not on what He has done for us and what He promises if we simply believe in Him.

Believing in Jesus Doesn't Mean Believing in Jesus

Second, Grudem diminishes the gospel by redefining faith to include good works.

There is a good reason why, as quoted above, Grudem believes the key question is, "How do I know *that I have truly believed?*" (p. 85). That is the key question for Grudem because he has redefined what it means to believe in Jesus.

Grudem explains what it means to believe in Jesus in various ways in this book. None of his explanations actually involve belief. Indeed, he mocks the idea that faith in Jesus is propositional:

> Some members of the Free Grace Alliance have also affirmed to me in personal correspondence and in private conversations that they do hold to faith in the *person* of Jesus Christ, not merely assent to facts about him…Many wonderful Free Grace Christians whom I know *pray* to Jesus; they don't pray to propositions about Jesus. In church they *worship* Jesus; they don't worship propositions about Jesus. In the

language of 1 Peter 1:8, they "love him" they
don't just love propositions about him (p. 102).

Really? Can anyone mindlessly pray to and worship
Jesus?

Can you have a content-less faith in Jesus? If faith is
not propositional, then it has no content.

How can you hallow Jesus' name without recalling
His character (e.g., good, loving, kind, gracious, eternal,
omniscient, omnipresent, omnipotent) and His works
(e.g., creation, the ten plagues, the parting of the Red
Sea, the conquest, Jesus' sinless life, healing the sick,
raising the dead, dying on the cross for our sins, His
marvelous teaching)? But each and every one of those
points is a proposition: Jesus is good. Jesus is loving.
Jesus is kind. Jesus is the Creator. Jesus raised the dead.

How can you love Jesus if you do not believe
anything about Him? Is love without content? Love
seems to be independent of belief for Grudem. But
the Apostle John says, "We love Him because He first
loved us" (1 John 4:19). Our love for Him is based on a
proposition: *He first loved us.* Calvary produces love in
us for Him (2 Cor 5:14; 1 John 3:16).

How can you believe in Jesus if you do not believe
propositions about Him? You cannot. All belief is
propositional.

Grudem sounds like he is saying that we do not need
to believe any propositions about Jesus. We do not need
to believe His promise of everlasting life to the believer.
We do not need to believe that He has the authority to
grant everlasting life. All we need to do is love Him,
commit to Him, confess Him, and obey Him. If we do

those things until we die, then we will make it into the kingdom.

Well, not quite.

Part of the problem of changing *believing* in Jesus to mean something else is that it is hard to remember all the things Grudem says are part of this redefined faith.

For example, Grudem says that believing in Jesus is repenting of one's sins (pp. 41-76) and heartfelt trust in the person of Christ (pp. 99-118). But repentance and heartfelt trust are complicated subjects in themselves.

Repentance includes renouncing, being sorry for, and turning from one's sins. Oh, and it is also committing yourself to obey Christ for the rest of your life.

Heartfelt trust in the person of Christ requires "total commitment to the one who is trusted" (p. 110). Repeatedly Grudem uses the language of postmodernity to speak of heartfelt trust as a "personal encounter" (pp. 106, 108, twice, 118), "personal interaction" (p. 108, 3 times), and "interpersonal interaction" (p. 107).

Grudem gives an illustration meant to explain what heartfelt trust in a person means:

> An airline passenger can believe that American Airlines has not had a fatal airplane crash in over ten years, with tens of thousands of flights completed successfully, and still experience great fear when he boards the plane. Believing those facts is still different than trusting the pilot himself. But if, when he boards the plane, he sees that the pilot happens to be his neighbor whom he has known for many years, then he

trusts the pilot himself, which is an example of trust in a person (p. 110).

Isn't this "heartfelt trust" in the neighbor pilot *propositional*? There are solid reasons why you believe your neighbor is a good pilot:

- He has been a good, responsible neighbor.
- He had an excellent military record before he joined American Airlines.
- He has flown for American Airlines for over twenty years.
- He has never had an accident.
- He is in outstanding health.

Believing these propositions gives you greater reason to board the plane. Grudem might call it "heartfelt trust," but this is just propositional faith. You believe your neighbor is an outstanding pilot.[1]

Over and over again the Lord Jesus Christ said that the one who believes in Him has everlasting life (cf. John 3:16-18; 5:24, 39-40; 6:35, 37, 39, 37; 11:25-27).

---

[1] Of course, Rain Man was right. Air travel is not 100% safe. A better illustration of saving faith would be something which is 100% certain. Even death and taxes are not 100% certain. Remember Enoch and Elijah. I suppose everything which is certain is something which God Himself guarantees. For example, I'm sure the Jewish people will not be destroyed because God has promised them a kingdom. I'm sure that mankind will not destroy the earth because the Lord guarantees the end-time events (rapture, tribulation, Millennium) before the new earth. And I'm sure that I have everlasting life and that anyone who believes in Jesus for that life has it as well. That is because the Lord Jesus is completely trustworthy. He is the Word! He is the way, the truth, and the life. He is telling the truth when He says, "he who believes in Me has everlasting life" (John 6:47).

But Grudem says something completely different. By redefining faith, Grudem misrepresents what the Lord Jesus and His Apostles taught. That is the second way in which Grudem diminishes the gospel.

Assurance Found Not by Looking to Jesus, But by Looking to Ourselves

Third, Grudem diminishes the gospel by basing assurance on man's performance, instead of on Jesus' promise.

Grudem is very concerned about false assurance. He has a whole chapter entitled, "False Assurance" (pp. 77-97). He is concerned that FGT is giving false assurance to people. He implies that people will end up spending eternity in the lake of fire because they were misled by FGT (p. 97).

How do Free Grace people mislead people about their eternal destiny? By telling people who believe in Jesus for their eternal salvation that they are born again. That, to him, is giving false assurance.

Pointing people to John 3:16 for assurance is wrong because John 3:16 doesn't mention the need to repent from one's sins (p. 78).

Showing people John 5:24 as a basis of assurance is folly because John 5:24 does not say, "faith without works is dead" (p. 79).

First John 5:9-13 leads to false assurance because it does not say that one who "keeps on sinning" will be eternally condemned (1 John 3:6, p. 81).

You can't get assurance from Eph 2:8-9 because you can't know if you have "truly believed" in Christ or not (p. 85).

Grudem believes that God does not want anyone
to be sure of his eternal destiny prior to death. Why?
Because he understands the various warning passages
in Scripture to be warnings about eternal condemnation
to the believer who does not persevere. In his view the
warnings spur the elect to do the good works necessary
for them to be saved. Remember, faith alone cannot
save anyone according to Grudem's understanding
of Jas 2:14-17. For example, after quoting Jas 2:14-17
Grudem says, "If a person has no good works, if there is
no change in his life, then he has 'dead faith'—and verse
14 implies that that kind of faith cannot save a person"
(p. 80).

Read that last sentence again. When would a person
be saved eternally according to Grudem? When he
believes in Christ? Or when he believes in Christ plus
has good works and a changed life? Clearly Grudem says
that until a person has good works and a changed life he
has "dead faith," and thus he is not yet saved.

Works are needed to be saved. Perseverance to the
end of life in good works is necessary.

It is important for Grudem that he is not sure
where he is going when he dies. He must be afraid that
he might not persevere to the end. He must believe he
might not make it. And he thinks that it is important for
everyone to share his uncertainty.

See, for example, p. 89 where Grudem indicates
that "other verses base assurance on continuing in faith,
such as… 'if indeed we hold our original confidence to
the end' [Heb 3:15]…and 'if indeed you continue in the
faith, stable and steadfast, not shifting from the hope
of the gospel that you heard' [Col 1:22-23]." *If we base
our assurance on continuing in faith* as Grudem says,

then until we have continued to the end, we can't have assurance!

In his mind the only way we can safely make it into the kingdom is to live each day dangling over the abyss. So it is understandable that Grudem rails against Free Grace people who tell people that they can be sure, apart from their works. He thinks that leads to loose living, which in turns leads to the lake of fire. In his mind, because of false assurance, many Free Grace people do not have joy, do not understand the Bible, and do not have meaningful prayer lives (p. 78). Oppositely, his lack of certainty gives him joy, understanding of the Bible, and a meaningful prayer life.

At one point Grudem quotes me as saying "If saving faith is more than believing facts...it is impossible to be sure of your eternal destiny since you can't be sure that you believe in Christ" (p. 95). In the next paragraph he attempts to paraphrase what I believe, saying that I contend that "people who reject a Free Grace position are unable to have a confident assurance of their own salvation in this lifetime" (p. 95).

Did you catch the theological sleight of hand?

I spoke of being "*sure* of your eternal destiny *now*." He changed that into saying we can "have *a confident assurance* of [our] salvation *in this lifetime*." I spoke of being sure *today*. He spoke of having confident assurance *in this lifetime*.

That is the tragedy of Lordship Salvation. For them assurance is *confidence*, i.e., some degree of probability, but not certainty. And they say a high level of confidence is something we can't have *today*, but something we hope to achieve "in this lifetime." Grudem believes we can't have *certainty* until after we die.[2]

The reason why Grudem lacks certainty, and why Free Grace people have it, is because we base our assurance on what Jesus did and promised, while Grudem looks to what he has done and has promised to do. Ironically, although Grudem emphasizes heartfelt personal trust in Jesus, he apparently does not trust Jesus to guarantee his salvation.

Earlier, Grudem used an airline illustration. He compared saving faith not to believing in the pilot (and airline), but to having heartfelt trust in the pilot because he is our neighbor. Likewise, it is not enough to believe in Jesus, we're also supposed to place heartfelt trust in Jesus for our salvation.

Only, Grudem doesn't actually place heartfelt trust in Jesus for *his* salvation. In fact, he insists we can't just look to Jesus alone for assurance that He will safely get us to our destination.

In the illustration, Grudem believes we can be sure we will arrive safely at our destination if our neighbor is the pilot. But when it comes to assurance of everlasting life, Grudem says we can't be certain we will arrive safely in Jesus' kingdom if Jesus is our pilot. Why? Because, for Grudem, it doesn't depend on Jesus and what He promised. It depends on us and how we perform.

Do you see the difference?

---

[2] Of course, the Twelve were sure. They were guaranteed to sit on twelve thrones and rule with Christ (Matt 19:28). The seventy were told to rejoice that their names were written in heaven (Luke 10:20). Clement was told his name is in the Book of Life (Phil 4:3). Why could these people be certain, but we can't? Did the Lord give out false assurance?

On the plane our role is passive. We simply believe the pilot and we're sure we'll make it. But in Christianity, according to Grudem, we are not mere passengers. We must be active participants the entire trip, i.e., our entire lives. In order to make it to our destination, we can't just trust Jesus to take us there. We must repeatedly turn from our sins, confess Christ, submit to Him, obey Him, love the brethren, and demonstrate a markedly changed life.

The good news of Jesus Christ is that He died on the cross for our sins, was buried, and rose from the dead on the third day so that whoever simply believes in Him has everlasting life which can never be lost. Assurance of everlasting life is the promise of the gospel. Grudem diminishes the gospel by changing certainty now into the hope of probability in the future.

The Word of God Is Replaced with the Traditions of Men

Fourth, Grudem diminishes the gospel by allowing tradition to trump Scripture.

Authors typically show emphasis by their first and last words. In *5 Ways* Grudem's first chapter deals with the traditions of men. He says that FGT diminishes the gospel because it is not consistent with Reformed tradition. Why bring this up at all, let alone in the first chapter? It is the Word of God that gives us our marching orders, not the traditions of men. Didn't our Lord Jesus contend all throughout His ministry with the traditions of men? The traditions of the Sadducees and Pharisees contradicted the Word of God.

Chapter 5, the last chapter, presumably deals with the Word of God. However, in reality, even in the eleven passages which Grudem discusses in that chapter, he relies upon traditional interpretations of those verses.[3] He does not actually exegete any of the eleven texts. Why? Because for him Reformed theology has been proven true. So if you wish to know what a given passage means, look it up in a Reformed commentary. Don't study the passage for yourself. If you do, you might end up coming to some interpretation that is inconsistent with Reformed thought.

Funny, but that is the exact same argument that Roman Catholics and Orthodox have always used.

It diminishes the Good News of Jesus Christ if we follow the traditions of men and not the Word of God.

The Judgment Seat of Christ Is Another Name for the Great White Throne Judgment

Fifth, Grudem diminishes the gospel by confusing eternal life with eternal rewards.

A key aspect of FGT is the distinction between the Judgment Seat of Christ (the Bema) and the Great White Throne Judgment (GWTJ). To say it another way, we distinguish between everlasting life, which is a free gift received by faith alone, apart from works, and eternal rewards, which are earned by work done for Christ.

Grudem diminishes the gospel by making entering Christ's kingdom a reward for work done.

---

[3] See especially pp. 137-40 in *5 Ways*. Grudem says, "This pattern of idiosyncratic, eccentric interpretations, as illustrated in the verses above, continues nearly everywhere one looks in Free Grace literature" (p. 137).

All through the book Grudem interprets eternal rewards passages as if they were about gaining everlasting life (e.g., see pp. 80-81, 86-87, 89, 130-32, 139). For a particularly egregious example, note how at the end of Chapter 5, after he has discussed the eleven key passages he wished to discuss, he lambasts me for my understanding of Gal 6:7-9 as referring to the Bema and eternal rewards, not the GWTJ and eternal salvation. Tom Schreiner and I were two contributors to a *Four Views* book on the role of works in the final judgment by Zondervan.[4] Grudem cites Schreiner's response to my article in that book:

> What could ever convince Wilkin and those who support him that they are wrong? If the text says good works are necessary for eternal life [and here Schreiner is discussing Galatians 6:7-9, where Paul says that "the one who sows to the Spirit will from the Spirit reap eternal life"], then (according to Wilkin) the eternal life is different from the eternal life that brings salvation...No evidence could ever be adduced that would prove the contrary. For even if the Bible were to say, "good works are necessary for eternal life and to escape hell," it seems that Wilkin would say, "eternal life and hell have different meaning here" (p. 139).[5]

Once again, Grudem fails to explain why I say that Gal 6:7-9 deals with the Bema and not the GWTJ.

---

[4] Alan P. Stanley, editor, *Four Views on the Role of Works at the Final Judgment* (Grand Rapids, MI: Zondervan, 2013), 44.
[5] This is p. 55 in *Four Views*.

Grudem does not discuss the evidence I cite. Nor does Schreiner, whom he quotes.[6] In addition to being intellectually unfair, that practice is also spiritually deceptive.

Did you notice that Schreiner boldly and openly says, "good works are necessary for eternal life"? Does that statement exalt or diminish the gospel of Jesus Christ? And did you notice that Grudem cites that statement favorably?[7]

If you look at the *Four Views* book, you will see that I argue as follows: In Gal 6:7-9 Paul says that eternal life is *earned* by reaping what we sow. In Eph 2:8-9 the same author says, "For by grace you have been saved through

---

[6] Schreiner does wrongly say, "Ephesians 2:8-9 does not speak of eternal life," *Four Views*, 54. But actually it does. Verse 5, which precedes and mirrors v 8, says, "even when we were dead in trespasses, [God] made us alive together with Christ (by grace you have been saved)." Made alive unmistakably means *regenerated, given everlasting life.* But since that doesn't fit Schreiner and Grudem's theology, neither notices that.

[7] Grudem does say in footnote 31 on p. 139 that, "Schreiner is not arguing that good works are necessary for justification but rather that 'the faith that saves is never alone' because it is always accompanied by good works, and numerous New Testament passages such as Galatians 6:7-9 point to the conclusion." As my beloved Dad would have said, "That is malarkey." Schreiner is arguing that good works are necessary for everlasting life. Did Grudem even read the book? If so, where does *Schreiner* make this clarification? Why not quote him instead of putting words in his mouth? Did Grudem read Schreiner's book, *The Race Set Before Us*? In that book Schreiner repeatedly says that good works are necessary for eternal life. Talk about criticizing someone else for something you do. Grudem chastises me for the way I interpret the words of Gal 6:7-9 as being totally contrary to what the words themselves mean, and then he tries to make Schreiner say something other than "good works are necessary for eternal life." In addition, Grudem accepts without explanation that Gal 6:7-9 is saying that we reap what we sow. Paul isn't saying that eternal life is a free gift, but that if we have it, we will overflow in good works. He is saying that we will reap eternal life for work done if we sow to the Spirit and not to the flesh.

faith. And this is not from yourselves; it is the gift of God, not from works, so that no one may boast." This is in a large chart in the *Four Views* book.[8] I don't see how Grudem missed it. Paul defines *you have been saved* in v 5 as meaning, "you have been made alive." That is, you have been given everlasting life.

As I point out in *Four Views*, sowing and reaping are unmistakably farming language—the language of hard work (Matt 13:3, 4, 24, 25, 27, 31, 37; Mark 4:3, 4, 14; Luke 8:5; 19:21-22 [in a Bema passage]; John 4:36-37; 2 Cor 9:6 [Bema passage])—not the language of a free gift. If Gal 6:7-9 means that "good works are necessary for eternal life," then Eph 2:8-9 is a lie. Oh, and so is John 3:16. And John 5:24. And John 5:39-40. And 6:28-29. And John 11:25-27. And Acts 16:31. And Gal 2:16. And Rom 4:4-5. And Titus 3:5. And Rev 22:17. The entire Bible collapses if a multitude of verses teach that eternal salvation is not of works and yet one passage teaches that it is of works.

My solution is to explain the seeming discrepancy. Most of the passages in the New Testament which speak of everlasting life refer to it as *a present possession*. However, there are three texts which refer to it as a *possible future reality*, not a present reality. Those texts are Matt 19:29 ("Everyone who has left houses or brothers...for My name's sake, shall...inherit eternal life"), 1 Tim 6:12, 19 ("take hold of eternal life"), and Gal 6:7-9. Is it sloppy exegesis to note that a future tense is used in Gal 6:8 ("will reap eternal life"), but a perfect tense is used in Eph 2:8 ("you have been saved")? I think it is sloppy exegesis to fail to note the difference. And

---

[8] *Four Views*, 41.

it is certainly sloppy for Grudem to fail to discuss the evidence.

In answer to Schreiner and Grudem's challenge, I plead guilty. There is no verse anywhere in the Bible that says that having everlasting life right now requires anything other than faith in Christ. Not one.

I wish that people like Grudem would deal with what the text says and not with what their tradition says the text should mean.

If the Bema is another name for the GWTJ, which is what Schreiner says in his response to my chapter in *Four Views,*[9] then the Lord Jesus Christ did not buy everlasting life for us. We buy it for ourselves. If that isn't diminishing the gospel, what is?

Conclusion

I hold no animosity toward Wayne Grudem (or other Lordship Salvation proponents). I have heard him speak, but I do not know him personally.

---

[9] *Four Views, 52.* Schreiner says, "When I first encountered solutions like Wilkin proposes regarding the judgment, I found it impossible to remember in the judgment passages whether the judgment of believers or unbelievers was in view." Schreiner was trained by Earl Radmacher at Western Seminary. That Schreiner can no longer remember what Radmacher taught him is sad. That he pretends that my view is impossibly complicated is doubly sad. Here is a clue: If the judgment in question is giving out degrees of rewards for works done, that is the Bema. If the judgment is giving out degrees of torment for work done, that is the GWTJ. Of course, even at the GWTJ the basis of eternal condemnation is not works done (or not done), but the failure of having one's name in the Book of Life (Rev 20:15) because one did not believe in Jesus for everlasting life in his lifetime (John 11:26).

I am offended, however, by what he says about me and about FGT. He says that we diminish the gospel of the Lord Jesus Christ.

Based on *5 Ways*, I'm not sure if Grudem has ever believed in Jesus for everlasting life. I'm confident that he has turned from his sins, that he has submitted himself to Christ, that he is doing his best to obey Him, and that he feels close to Christ. But has he ever believed that by faith in Him he has everlasting life which can never be lost? I hope so. I imagine it is quite likely that he believed the promise of life before he drifted off into his current position.

If he is a believer who has lost his way, then he will be at the Bema and he will give an account to Christ for what he has written in *5 Ways* and for all that he has said and written. I realize that holds true for me, too. I take very seriously the warning of James. Grudem mentions many warnings. But he didn't choose to mention this one: "Let not many of you become teachers, my brethren, for as such we will incur a stricter judgment" (Jas 3:1).

If Grudem is right, then I will either be in the lake of fire forever (since I do not believe what he calls the gospel and he says we must continue to believe his gospel until we die to make it into the kingdom) or, if I somehow get a pass on my false gospel, I'll have a rough time at the Bema.

One final comment. Grudem points out that Free Grace authors almost never publish with major publishers. He says,

> Nearly all Free Grace publications are published
> by their own organizations or are self-published

by the individual authors. With the exception of the book by Zane Hodges, *Absolutely Free!*, [*sic*] which was published by Zondervan as an alternative viewpoint to the simultaneous publication of John MacArthur's *The Gospel According to Jesus: What Is Authentic Faith?*, [*sic*] anniversary edition. (Grand Rapids, MI: Zondervan, 2008),[10] and a 2009 Kregel book by Charles Bing that is now out of print,[11] I am not aware of any Free Grace book that has been published by a recognized, mainstream evangelical academic publisher (such as Zondervan, Baker, Crossway, InterVarsity Press, P & R, B & H, or others). This means that (with two exceptions) their publications have not made it through the rigorous editorial vetting process that established publishers undertake before they will publish a manuscript (p. 138, note 30).[12]

Grudem is mistaken. There have been many Free Grace books published by major publishers, though they did not necessarily use the expression *Free Grace*.

---

[10] Actually the book published at approximately the same time as *Absolutely Free!* was the 1988 edition of *The Gospel According to Jesus*. The 2008 edition, which Grudem cites, was published 19 years after Hodges wrote *Absolutely Free!*

[11] Actually that book, *Simply by Grace: An Introduction to God's Life-Changing Gift* (Grand Rapids, MI: Kregel, 2009), is still in print..

[12] It is odd that Grudem gives full bibliographic information for MacArthur, but only a partial title and no publication information for Hodges, and not even a title for Bing.

Zane C. Hodges's book *The Hungry Inherit* was first published in 1972 by Moody Press, then re-released by Multnomah Press in 1980.

Grudem evidently forgot, but he earlier cited a Zondervan book which I co-authored called *Four Views on the Role of Works at the Final Judgment*, edited by Alan Stanley. I presented the Free Grace view in that book.

Charles Ryrie published many books defending FGT which were published by major publishers. *A Survey of Bible Doctrine* and *Balancing the Christian Life* were published by Moody Press. *So Great Salvation* was published by Victor Press.

Millions of *The Ryrie Study Bible*, published by Moody Press, are in print, and Ryrie's notes defend a Free Grace perspective.

Another very popular study Bible is *The Nelson Study Bible*. Earl Radmacher was the general editor. It too presents Free Grace views.

Thomas Nelson published a major one volume commentary on the New Testament by William MacDonald with contributions by Art Farstad. That commentary presents Free Grace views.

Lewis Sperry Chafer defended FGT in a book entitled *Salvation*, published by Zondervan.

Logos (now FaithLife) published a course on FGT (TH 265) that I taught.

Tony Evans has written many Free Grace books by Moody Press, Thomas Nelson, Harvest House, Crossway Books, and many others.

John Hart published several books with Moody Press which defend a Free Grace perspective.

Gary Derickson published a major Free Grace commentary on 1-3 John with Lexham Press, the publishing arm of Logos/Faithlife.

A Free Grace book entitled *Salvation* was published by Word Publishing. This was part of the Swindoll Leadership Library. The author was Earl Radmacher.

Charles Stanley, with the help of his son, Andy Stanley, wrote *Eternal Security*, a powerful defense of FGT. It was published by Thomas Nelson.

Michael Eaton's book *No Condemnation: A New Theology of Assurance* takes a Free Grace stand on the issue of assurance. It was published by InterVarsity Press.

Many more examples could be cited.

Grudem has not done his research.

Even so, the main issue in terms of whether a book is ultimately a success is not whether it is released by a major publisher, nor even how many copies have been sold, but whether what has been written pleases the Lord Jesus Christ (2 Cor 5:9-10). If *5 Ways* pleases the Lord Jesus Christ, then it is an award-winning book, whether it is well received by the world or not. If *5 Ways* is a massive best seller and displeases the Lord Jesus Christ, then I'm sure Grudem would agree that it would be a terrible failure.

I earnestly hope that after reading my response to Grudem any Lordship Salvation followers who have never believed on the Lord Jesus Christ for everlasting life would do so. "He who hears My word and believes in Him who sent Me has everlasting life, shall not come into judgment, but has passed from death into life" (John 5:24). I long for Lordship Salvation people like Wayne Grudem to know the joy of being certain that they have everlasting life right now, that they will never come into judgment regarding their eternal destiny, and that they have already passed from death into life.

Conclusion

WAYNE GRUDEM IS AN established scholar of the first rank. He has degrees from Harvard (A.B.), Westminster (M.Div.), and University of Cambridge (Ph.D. in New Testament). His best-selling *Systematic Theology* has sold over 400,000 copies. He regularly publishes books with Crossway and Zondervan on a wide variety of subjects.

However, while Grudem is an expert in several theological fields, in *5 Ways* he addressed a subject he does not know very well. He knows Reformed Theology. But he doesn't know FGT, and it is evident in his book.

If you were evaluating FGT for yourself, where would you start? What would be your standard?

For Grudem, the standard was tradition and consensus theology. How does FGT stand up against the historic Protestants? From the very first chapter, Grudem did not center his discussion on the Bible.

Is that the right way to decide whether a theology is true?

If theology can be rejected by being inconsistent with the scholarly consensus, then FGT is *adokimos*, disapproved.

If theology can be rejected because it does not agree with Reformed theology, then FGT is kaput.

If quoting verses without any discussion proves your case, then FGT is dead in the water.

But, if theological truth is established by careful exegesis of the Word of God, then FGT has a chance.

Grudem does not carefully exegete the Word of God in *5 Ways*.

Most of the time he doesn't even try. He simply quotes verses and assumes that his point is proven.

That won't convince any who hold to FGT. We are committed Biblicists. Our standard is the Word of God. Our consciences are bound by that Word. If the Word says it, that settles it. But it takes effort to determine what the Word says. Proof-texting is not good enough. Assuming the truth of traditional Protestant interpretations is not good enough. We have been spoiled by men like Darby, MacIntosh, Chafer, Ryrie, Hodges, Thieme, and so many more who carefully defended what they were saying from God's Word.

I doubt that studious Reformed people will be convinced by Grudem's arguments either. If they come to *5 Ways* already believing in Lordship Salvation, then they might well leave with that view intact. But they will surely notice that Grudem does not try to explain why FGT believes what it does. Grudem does occasionally quote FGT authors. I hope that some Reformed readers will be curious enough to follow up on those quotes, and study FGT works for themselves, to come to their own conclusions about who has the better Biblical arguments.

I respect Wayne Grudem as a scholar and as one committed to pleasing the Lord Jesus Christ. However, *5 Ways* reveals some major blind spots in both his thinking and his understanding of God's Word. It was intellectually lazy for him not to at least summarize our arguments and explanations. That is not up to the standards of his other books.

Readers may be interested to know that I wrote a chapter-by-chapter, section-by-section response to John MacArthur's, *The Gospel According to Jesus* (*TGAJ*) called *A Gospel of Doubt*.[1] If you want to read further on this subject, I would recommend reading those two books.

Readers may be interested in my personal theological journey. In my youth, I held to extreme Arminian theology. I believed in sinless perfectionism as the condition for staying saved. Until age twenty I believed that once you were good enough to be saved (by repenting and committing your life to Christ over the course of years of spiritual pilgrimage), you had to live a sinless life to stay saved. Only by the grace of God did I learn the message of Eph 2:8-9 over five sessions with Warren Wilke, a Campus Crusade for Christ staff member at my college, U. C. Irvine.

My life was radically changed when I was set free from legalistic bondage, insecurity, and spiritual death. I went from pre-med to pre-ministry.

Since then, I have devoted my life to telling people about the free gift of everlasting life.

I have found that certainty of my eternal destiny drives me to give my all for Christ each day.

I'll be 66 this year. I could retire. But I hope to keep working full-time for many more years. I love telling

---

[1] Robert N. Wilkin, *A Gospel of Doubt: The Legacy of John MacArthur's* The Gospel According to Jesus (Denton, TX: Grace Evangelical Society, 2015).

people that everlasting life is a free gift which the Lord Jesus Christ gives to all who simply believe in Him for it.

If you lack certainty of your eternal destiny, would you pray about it? Would you ask God to show you if it is possible to know for sure you are eternally secure?

I recommend you read John's Gospel, one chapter per day, prayerfully. Pay attention to how Jesus evangelized. Note what He said. Note the promises He made about everlasting life. Who gets that life? On what condition? When do you get it—now or in the future? Can it be lost?

But whatever you do, *do not take the words of men as the basis of your faith.* The basis of your faith should be *the Word of God.* Don't base your eternal salvation on what Grudem or I say. Base it on the promise of the Lord Jesus Christ. So check out what He said. Carefully.

May God bless you as you seek the truth! Remember, He is a rewarder to those who diligently seek Him (Heb 11:6; Acts 17:11).

Scripture Index

Subject Index